Not Quite a Stranger

Not Quite a Stranger

Essays on Life in France

David Bouchier

ISBN: 1517543746
ISBN 13: 9781517543747
Library of Congress Control Number: 2015916230
CreateSpace Independent Publishing Platform
North Charleston, South Carolina

Also By David Bouchier

Peripheral Vision: Irregular Essays from Public Radio (2011)
A Few Well-Chosen Words (2007)
Writer at Work (2005)
The Song of Suburbia (2002)
The Cats and the Water Bottles and Other Mysteries of French Village Life (2002)
The Accidental Immigrant (1996)
Radical Citizenship (1986)
The Feminist Challenge (1984)
Idealism and Revolution (1978)

Contents

Preface

We are always outsiders in a strange land, but the experience that Mark Twain called "getting foreignized" is different for everyone. There are many ways of being abroad: as a resident or as a tourist, alone or *en famille*, independently or in the bubble of a tour bus or cruise ship. The vast majority of tourists put their faith in the mighty travel industry, which now reaches into the remotest corners of the earth. A well-organized tour eliminates problems of security and language, where to go and what to do. The interface between travelers and their foreign surroundings is as smooth as the operators can make it and, at its best, is very much like watching a documentary movie. Some companies include a dash of synthetic "adventure" in their trips, but never without a safety net.

The most dramatic travel books are written by lone explorers like Bruce Chatwin, Freya Stark, Paul Theroux, and Charles Montagu Doughty. They were real adventurers who exposed themselves nakedly to strange peoples and alarming cultures, so we don't have to. What we get from them is something close to the truth about the places they have seen. The memoirs of the average tourist are inevitably more like a review on Trip Advisor, composed in suburban tranquility after the event.

My own travels in the civilized and safe parts of the world have fallen between the extremes of tourism and adventure. But I have always loved the great spectacle called "abroad," and these essays on France and the French are affectionate snapshots from more than fifty years of travel and increasing familiarity. Like a good marriage, it gets better every year.

David Bouchier
Saint Quentin la Poterie, France,
2015

Introduction

"Every man has two countries, his own and France."
BENJAMIN FRANKLIN

*F*amily legend suggests that my father's great-great grandfather emigrated from France to England in 1804, the year that Napoleon proclaimed himself Emperor. So we have always had a this fragile connection, even though both my parents did their best to forget it. But for me France was always a second home of the imagination, until I could make it real.

The real France began for me in 1957, when I took my newly-acquired but very old motorcycle on the ferry from Dover. We landed in Calais, the bike was lifted out of the hold with a crane, and I rode into the devastation that was Calais a dozen years after the end of the war. Luckily I had grown up in London, so urban devastation was nothing new to me. It was raining hard as I took the narrow, slippery road towards Paris, delighted by the unfamiliar French cars that passed and the delinquent thrill that came from driving on the wrong side of the road.

When you cross a European frontier, everything changes – the language, the lifestyle and, in some mysterious way, even the landscape.

In the United States, just because they are more or less united, the traveler doesn't experience the same cultural shocks. You can cross from New York into Connecticut, for example, and not notice the difference for days, or even for years. When you cross from England to France you emerge into a completely different world.

In the cathedral town of Reims I decided to stop for the night and get some food, which was easier said than done. But in a side street I found a small restaurant with a brown-painted facade and dirty net curtains covering the windows. Ever since that cold wet evening I have favored French restaurants with brown painted facades and net curtains. I am happy to report that there are still plenty of them.

I parked my motorcycle, entered the steamy interior, and stood there dripping like the proverbial drowned rat, my glasses completely misted up. Madame took me in hand and sat me down and started to serve me food. I had worried about ordering in my rudimentary French, but no ordering was necessary. The menu of the evening was the menu, and it started with the most delicious leek and potato soup I have ever tasted, followed by a rich stew with beans that I later learned was called *Cassoulet*. For a boy who had grown up in the dreary suburbs of London in an era of food rationing this was already enough adventure to last a lifetime. I have never asked for anything more. To this day, when I think about escape I think first of France, and then of leek and potato soup.

Chapter 1

An Innocent Abroad

> *"We went to see the cathedral of Notre*
> *Dame. We had heard of it before."*
> MARK TWAIN, *THE INNOCENTS ABROAD*

*E*veryone expects a book about France to begin with Paris, and so it should. After my initial adventure in 1957 I was drawn back many times. Paris was a rather sad city in the fifties, but quickly rediscovered its former glittering style.

Paris is the number one destination in the world, but my intention was never to be a tourist. I had visited all the main "sights" in the first couple of weeks and felt no compulsion to see them again. My plan was to become a bohemian, and a great writer. Everything I had read suggested that being a bohemian and a great writer was just about the best career plan a young man could have. Such a life seemed to promise a great deal of fun and virtually no hard work.

In 1958 when between jobs I made my first serious escape attempt, and headed for Paris with a small hoard of francs and several blank notebooks that I hoped to fill with searing and revealing prose, and several fountain pens. Much to my delight I found lodging in a literal left bank garret right beside the Pantheon, in a building called the *Hotel des Grands Hommes*. The name appealed to me, and the place is now a rather grand hotel, although in those days it certainly was not.

So I was able to experience Paris as so many had done before as a stage set for the performance of being a bohemian and a great writer, or at least a future yet-to-be-discovered great writer. I haunted the Luxembourg Gardens and the maze of streets around the Boulevard Saint Michel, and spent a lot of time reading in cafés and in the Bibliotheque Buffon. I learned to drink wine and wear corduroy and dark glasses at all times.

Writing was a different matter. I suffered from the universal problem of the young writer: having absolutely nothing to say. All my experience was secondhand, and the intellectual circles of Paris where I hoped to find friends and perhaps mentors were closed to me. As I became ever so slightly more cosmopolitan I realized what an invisibly low place I occupied in the intellectual hierarchy. Real writers and students felt far too grand to waste their time with young pretenders of my type.

So my notebooks filled up slowly and my francs ran out quickly. Soon I had to find a job, which was not an easy matter because I had no work permit. My sole qualification was a couple of years working on a motorcycle magazine, and eventually I found temporary work in a remote part of the 13th arrondissement, repairing bicycles and numerous examples of the popular but unreliable VéloSolex motorized cycle. This was not why I had come to Paris, although there was something authentically Orwellian about it.

The romantic side of Paris was even harder to find. The city was full of stunningly beautiful girls, as it still is. But the local beauties were cut off from me by language, and those who spoke English, like the Dutch, the

Germans and the Scandinavians, only wanted to practice their French on the pretty French boys, and not on me in my faux bohemian corduroys. Never have I felt the barriers of language so painfully.

In the end my money ran out with my luck, and I returned to England only to revisit Paris again and again over the next fifty years. Having abandoned my youthful fantasies I was now able to enjoy the city for what it is – a superb urban spectacle. Of course it is full of Parisians, who are more combative and opinionated even than New Yorkers. There's also the diabolical traffic, the wall-to-wall tourists and the intimidating restaurant waiters. Every successive Mayor of Paris and French President launches a campaign to encourage Parisians to be nice to their visitors. This has been about as successful as a campaign urging Americans to be nice to Iran.

But I am used to all that, and to all the other departures from standard American culture. I don't want or expect French waiters to smile at me, and say "Bonjour, my name is Jacques, I will be your server today." Paris is not Disneyland and France is not Iowa. That's precisely why so many Americans go there every year. Oscar Wilde said: "When good Americans die, they go to Paris," which probably explains the long lines of elderly Midwesterners outside the Louvre. They just booked their flights in advance, to get the extra discount. When the sun shines, as it does rather rarely, there is no place like Paris. Nowhere are there more places to eat and drink outdoors, right in the middle of street life. Nowhere can you find more art and architectural treasures so beautifully displayed.

I always feel slightly inferior in Paris, which is another good reason for going. It's such a cultural and intellectual powerhouse, and the people have such style. Who can compete with them? Certainly not I. This inferiority complex began when I went to live there at the age of eighteen, and nothing has happened to change it. My favorite left-bank café is now a MacDonald's, but the old magic is still there. Whenever I walk down the Boulevard Saint Michel it is déjà vu all over again. Paris is a place of imaginary romantic memories as much as a place of real boulevards and galleries and insane taxi drivers.

The following ten essays are about modern Paris, a less scruffy and more commercialized city than the one I first encountered fifty years ago, but still one of the grandest places in the world.

Chapter 2

French France

*F*rance is still very French, in case you were worried, and Paris is still more French than anywhere else in spite of the annual invasion of thirty million visitors. The French seem to hang on to their habits and traditions more tenaciously than other nationalities.

One habit that has not changed is their annoying habit of speaking French at all hours of the day, and expecting others to do the same. My lifelong battle with the French language shows no sign of being won, now or ever. Paris is particularly difficult because everyone there imagines that their French is perfect, and they're wrong. The city is a cacophony of exotic accents: Moroccan, Senegalese, Vietnamese, Provençal, and dozens of others. Anyone speaking standard French out of a textbook doesn't stand much chance of understanding or communicating anything.

My weakness, like that of so many English speakers, is gender. Why should it be *La France* (feminine) the country, and *Le français* (masculine) the language? It makes no sense at all. And why should nouns and verbs always have to agree? The sacred French principle of *la liberté* (feminine) suggests that nouns and verbs should go their own ways and, when I speak, they usually do.

Europe already has a universal food, pizza; a universal juvenile headgear, the backward baseball cap; and a universal television hero, Bart Simpson. From 2002 the nations of the European Community had a universal currency. The next logical step must surely be a universal language that will make the union of Europe as solid as that of the United States.

A lot of people, especially the British, want that language to be English, but I'd vote for Italian. After all, it is the direct descendant of the Latin that was spoken all over Europe two thousand years ago. It is the language of Dante, the language of Grand Opera, and the familiar language of a million American restaurant menus. Italian is so clear, logical, and pronounceable, that I believe even I could learn it. If Italian became the universal language of Europe I might stand a better chance of being understood in France.

But in the matter of language Paris is still as inexorably French as it was when I first came there as a teenager. Other things have changed. What I enjoyed most in the 1950s and 1960s was the life of the cafés. There are still dozens of busy cafés in the almost-trendy tenth *arrondissement* where we lived for a while. But the traditional café is under threat, like so many other French institutions. The long lunch hour is shorter, the homicidal taxi driver is almost but not quite extinct, adultery is out of fashion, and cafés all over France are closing at the rate of about two a day. Nothing can replace them.

English pubs are suffering the same fate. It's the smoking ban, of course, which came into effect in France in 2008. Smoking was as essential to the French café as wine or Pastis, but now it's gone and many of the customers have gone with it. I'm a non-smoker myself, but I used to love the thick atmosphere of a French café where I could inhale my year's ration of nicotine in an hour, and free. Now the air is clear inside, if not outside, and social life is the poorer for it.

Paris is still a highly literary and intellectual city. On the subways you see more people engaged with serious books, and even musical scores, than with tabloids or iPods. And I think that the famous French intellectuals have given me a way out of my language dilemma. Twentieth century *enfant terrible* Jacques Derrida and his many followers, all of whom were very much smarter than I, have pointed out just what a slippery thing language is. Words do not describe the real world, they argue. Almost any arrangement of words can be taken to mean almost anything. Consider, for example, this sentence from the philosopher G.E.Moore: "It's raining outside, but I don't believe that it is." What do you make of that? Probably nothing, but it's just the sort of thing I might say in French. So that's all right then, the philosophers are on my side. My French may be just about perfect, or not. Whatever I say in that or any other language may make sense, or not. As my wife said, rather unkindly: "*Quoi de neuf*": *W*hat else is new?

Chapter 3

Squeezing into Paris

We don't usually live in a small city apartment, or cook in a kitchen the size of a closet, or sleep in the kind of narrow, lumpy bed favored by French apartment owners. The metaphor of ferrets in a sack comes to mind. But when we are in Paris we have to downsize our expectations, at least as far as housing is concerned, and live the way most Parisians do.

Our rented apartment was in an up and coming *quartier* near the Canal Saint-Martin. The people on the street were shamelessly multi-ethnic, as were the stores and restaurants. You could sample most of the cuisines of the world within a radius of half a mile or so. It was a lively area, a bit like the East Village in New York or Camden Town in London.

In keeping with the liveliness of the area the apartment was secured behind three different locked doors requiring an access code and two complicated keys. These nineteenth century apartment blocks are very handsome, but they do have drawbacks. The lobby and stairwells had those timed light switches familiar to every visitor to France that illuminate the scene for about twelve seconds and then plunge you back into darkness. The old wood floors creaked and there were strict rules about noise after 10 p.m., so at night we crept around like cat burglars in stocking feet. But everyone else seemed to obey the noise regulation, so we did too. It led to early nights.

The elevator was about the size of a suitcase. The sign inside said "Three Persons, 223 kilograms," which is 490 pounds, or 163 pounds per person, without luggage. This is obviously not meant for Americans, or English people for that matter. Two of us can barely squeeze in. The elevator might just hold three very thin *Parisiennes* with very tiny shopping bags. In fact my new theory about why the people in this city are so thin is that most of them live in apartments where you can't get a decent sized bag of food into the elevator.

For this reason it was necessary to shop every day, just the way my mother used to do. Another reason, of course, was fresh bread. We had an award-winning *boulangerie* or baker's shop almost opposite, which always had a line of customers out the door during the odd hours when it was open. This daily shopping, though tedious in a way, meant that we got to know the neighborhood and the shopkeepers, and at least some of our neighbors.

I liked being in the apartment on a winter evening when the windows all around the courtyard lit up one after another, like one of those TV game shows. When all the windows were lit the message was complete, and it read: "Time for dinner." Nobody seemed to worry much about drapes, so after dark it was a multi-screen show about other people's lives and cooking habits. I was quite shocked to see how much pre-prepared food the French are using these days. Meanwhile they could observe our lives. It was certainly a change from the private world of the suburbs.

So in Paris, improbable as it seems, we rediscovered the virtues of the simple life, and of economy. We made the most of the modest resources we had. Who needs a big suburban house when there is a whole city to live in?

Chapter 4

Le Canal Saint-Martin

*I*t is amazing how quickly we can take possession of a place. A hotel room, a neighborhood, a village, or even a city is likely to be labeled "ours" after we've been living in it for a few weeks, or even a few days. I suspect that it is this human instinct to claim and defend territory that has caused most of the trouble in the world for the past few thousand years.

But biology is destiny, and we were happy to return to "our" neighborhood in Paris after spending The Holidays in England. It was reassuring to see the rather scruffy streets and shops just as we'd left them, the elegant old buildings being slowly restored as the area moves up-market, and the centerpiece of it all, the Canal Saint-Martin that gives its name to the neighborhood, or *le quartier* as the French prefer to call it in their Gallic way.

For me the Canal Saint-Martin was one of the pleasures of living in the tenth *arrondissement*. I loved the fact that, in the crowded heart of the city, the canal opened everything up. One minute you were in narrow, dark streets, and the next you were beside the canal with its great sweep of water and sky. Like a park, it was an antidote to city claustrophobia. So this was where we took our daily walk or bike ride under the bare plane trees, stopping by the locks like the idlers we were to watch barges making their slow way through, and perhaps, if we felt more than usually self-indulgent, stopping at one of the many cafés too. It had become "our" canal.

Before it was ours the Canal Saint-Martin belonged to Napoleon, who ordered it built in 1802 to speed the movement of goods through the middle of Paris. It's an impressive piece of nineteenth century engineering, with nine locks, each one an entertainment in itself, that drop the water level a total of seventy-four feet in just under three miles. For many decades this was a gritty, working class area, *terra incognita* for tourists. But about twenty years ago it began to change, and now it is something of a magnet for so-called "bobos" or bourgeois bohemians. There's even a Café Bobo, as well as galleries, art centers, and an increasing number of boutique stores selling very strange clothes at ridiculous prices. The area has been written up in *The New York Times* travel section which is the ultimate guarantee of its trendiness.

The old *quartier* is still here, under the shiny surface of the new shops. There's even a kind of romanticism about the bad old days, captured in a book of beautiful black and white photographs showing the era when tramps or *clochards* were harnessed like animals to haul the barges, and the canal was nothing but a rough and tough commercial highway with no charm whatsoever. Songs have been written about it, and a lot of local people resent the bourgeois invasion that is transforming their old *quartier*.

The most famous building along the canal is the *Hotel du Nord*, not because it is a thing of beauty but because it featured in a romantic film of the same name in 1938. Tourists came to look at the façade of the *Hotel du Nord*, and perhaps to have a drink in the bar, and marvel at the picturesque street life. Then they headed back to the more familiar territory of the Louvre and the Eiffel tower. But we stayed right there in the tenth *arrondissement*, beside the Canal Saint Martin. After all, it was "our" neighborhood.

Chapter 5

Intellectualism for Dummies

One of the unique features of Paris is the permanent open-air book sale along the banks of the Seine. It's so famous that it is actually listed as a World Heritage site. But the *bouquinistes* as the booksellers are called, are in trouble with the mayor. They are selling too few antique books and too many tourist souvenirs. The rising tide of plastic Eiffel Towers threatens to swamp this ancient literary marketplace. I've never really understood the appeal of plastic Eiffel Towers, or plastic Empire State Buildings or Leaning Towers of Pisa for that matter. But they sell much better than books, so I seem to be out of step with the rest of humanity as usual.

There are still many fine bookstores in Paris, but the stock is not as highbrow as you might imagine. *Les Nuls* have invaded the bookstores in a big way. *Les Nuls* means essentially "useless" or "stupid." In other words the French have their own range of instruction books on everything for dummies, including one with the grandiose title *Culture for Dummies*, which presumably covers everything, like Diderot's famous *Encyclopaedia*.

I find these "Dummies" books as puzzling as the plastic Eiffel Towers. I suppose the ironic titles help to diminish the fear of failure. Years ago there was a splendid collection of books, also with yellow covers, called the "Teach Yourself" series. They offered just about every subject from languages to aeronautical engineering, and they weren't embarrassing to read in public. Teaching yourself is an active, praiseworthy activity. Being a passive Dummy, an Idiot, or a *Nul*, it seems to me, is not.

French movies are another clue that our preconceptions about Gallic culture need to be adjusted. My wife was doing some research on French popular movies so I saw more than a hundred of them, under protest. These were the films that have been big box office hits in France but never make it to the United States, and they were dreadful. If movies are anything to go, by the French are attracted by really (really, really) silly comedies, sentimental tales of family life, and excruciating coming of age sagas, plus the usual fantasies of sex and extreme violence. If you imagine, as I did, that the French spend their evenings watching ultra-sophisticated New Wave movies, think again. The average French movie makes Batman look like a work of high culture.

So where do we get the idea that inside every Frenchman is a Jean Paul Sartre or Jean-Luc Godard, or that inside every French woman a Simone de Beauvoir or Marguerite Duras? It may be the black clothes and long scarves that make so many passersby look like creative artists, or it may simply be the result of several centuries of propaganda claiming that the French are smarter than anyone else. Either way it's an illusion, although an enjoyable one.

Genuine French intellectuals do exist, of course, and they make the rest of us feel like dummies. Just try to read a book by Michel Houellebecq, or dabble in the philosophical world of Jacques Derrida.

A migraine is guaranteed, probably with a stomach upset into the bargain. But that's fine because their work isn't meant for us, it's meant for them. These are the secrets of their tribe, and outsiders have no business trying to understand them. As for the rest of the French, I hate to tell you this but they are almost exactly as intellectual as us.

Chapter 6

Paris Style

The young men of Paris seem always to be on an invisible stage. Even adolescents choose their clothes with care, and wear them with the consciousness of being seen. They have perfected the insouciant gesture with a cigarette, or a cell phone, or an idly crossed leg at a café table. Their body language is self-confidently eloquent, and their hair is usually a work of art. In short they have adopted and adapted the style secrets of young French women, who seem (perhaps for this reason) to have abandoned them. It's as if the vanity of these young peacock males has used up all the available oxygen, leaving the females gasping for air.

In the United States young men could scarcely be more different, more natural, less self-conscious. There are two main styles, or anti-styles: the well-muscled, clean cut athletic type, loud and confident, and the defiant slob, monosyllabic and unsociable. Neither has any pretentions to fashion, and we may imagine that, in general, young American men do not constantly observe themselves in a mental mirror, or they would do something drastic about their clothes. Here, the roles of the sexes have not changed. Women are still expected to display the fine feathers, although not all of them use their ornithological advantage to good effect.

I confess that I have no business writing about style at all because I never had any myself. To the best of my recollection my clothes were only in fashion once, in about nineteen sixty-two, and that was largely by accident. On the other hand I do admire style, and felt rather jealous of young men in Paris. Of course I'm too old for skin tight jeans, and shoes that are shaped entirely unlike my feet, and I can't use my cell phone without getting out a magnifying glass to see the buttons, which rather spoils the elegant gesture. But I thought I might do something about my hair, which settled into its present non-style in about 1956 and has never changed, except by diminishing in quantity.

The tenth *arrondissement* where we were living, offered good news and bad news. On the one hand it was a major hairdressing center, because there is a big hairdressing school in the district. On the other hand most of these establishments catered to people of African heritage, and offered mainly dreadlocks, braids, or corn rows. I don't have the face or the raw material for any of these. Finally I chose Marcel, a unisex hairdresser who turned out to have Florida connections. He promised to make my hair more Parisian, which was disturbing in so far as Marcel's own hair was so very strange that it could get me ostracized or arrested at home on Long Island. As it turned out, after a great deal of careful cutting, brushing and the application of mysterious chemicals, my hair came out looking very much the way it has since 1956. I guess it's been that way too long to be "styled."

It does no good to try to be younger than one's age so, after this unsatisfactory experiment with hair, I left my wardrobe unimproved. This way I fit in perfectly with the decidedly un-stylish French men of my own age, who are either square or round, dusty black or dark brown, and who wear sensible shoes. Forty years on, with any luck, all those stylish young men will look exactly like us.

Chapter 7

The Past in a Box

An afternoon at a Museum or gallery is not necessarily my idea of fun. In a big museum the dead past weighs heavily on my spirits, and ignorance of lost civilizations weighs heavily on my mind. A museum is a waste of time unless you already know something about the history of the things you are looking at. Otherwise it's just a meaningless jumble of stuff.

Art galleries too, even the best of them, can be oppressive. There's something unsettling and inappropriate about displaying many works of art side by side, when each was created to be enjoyed separately. My college art history teacher used to take us to the National Gallery in London, which has thousands of paintings. She would lead us to one picture, tell us to study it for half an hour, and then we would leave. It worked for me, and it serves as a handy excuse on some occasions.

Back in the days when my wife and I traveled a great deal I was steered into every museum and gallery on the planet, or so it seemed to me. Sometimes I would feign illness, or blindness, or that useful malady called Stendhal's Syndrome that produces mental collapse in the presence of great art, but it never did me any good. We went to museums that nobody else had ever heard of, or found, tiny museums in the back streets of undistinguished towns in obscure countries, that were astonished to get a foreign visitor at all, let alone two. So I know something about museums.

Paris is the world center for first class museums and galleries, and here is one of my favorites - the splendid *Musée d'Orsay*. It is not as huge and daunting as the Louvre or the Metropolitan in New York, nor does the *Musée d'Orsay* look or feel like a traditional museum, for the very good reason that it is a converted railway station, a superb and original piece of recycling. Like Grand Central in New York the *Musée d'Orsay* has become a work of art in itself, with the difference that it also houses a shifting kaleidoscope of special art exhibitions as well as a permanent collection. There's no chance of getting bored by repetition here, although you might be bored (and frozen) by the long outdoor lines to buy tickets.

Naturally I have my least favorite museums in Paris, one of which is almost brand new: the *Musée du Quai Branly* not far along the Seine from the *Musée d'Orsay*. It is a collection of primitive art, although know I shouldn't say that. The politically correct terms are "first arts," or "indigenous arts." But old habits, like old art forms, die hard. We visited the *Branly* by way of honoring one hundredth anniversary of the birth of the great anthropologist Lévi-Strauss, who had nothing to do with blue jeans. It is ugly. On the outside it looks like a crashed space station. Inside it is disorienting and unpleasant, with a labyrinth of twisting corridors and ramps, and all the exhibits (which are mysterious and beautiful) shown in semi-darkness, presumably to mimic the darkness of the primitive world. This was a big political issue when the museum opened, and it should be. Even I know that the sun sometimes shone in the primitive world.

Architecture like this makes me feel old and hopelessly conservative, like Prince Charles, but what can I do? It's an instinctive reaction.
I don't want or expect every museum to look like a Greek temple. The
Tate Modern in London, which was built in the shell of an old power
station, is brilliant. But I don't like to be taunted by an architect. My
tastes may be primitive, but I hope I can tell the difference between
style and self-indulgence.

Chapter 8

The Secretive Gourmet

An eighteenth century French social critic with the splendid name of Charles-Louis de Secondat, baron de La Brède et de Montesquieu, said this about eating in Paris: "Lunch kills half of Paris, and supper kills the other half." There is some slight exaggeration in this statement, but only slight. Three hundred years after Montesquieu, the traditional French meal is still a digestive challenge.

The French have an international reputation for fine food, just as the British are known far and wide for the awfulness of theirs. These stereotypes are not as accurate as they used to be. You can eat badly in France, and superbly in Britain. But the French have traditionally cared a great deal about food, while the British have taken pride in their simple meat-and-potatoes diet, which is why the French call them *Les Rosbifs* (literally the roast beefs). A visit to any French local market compared to its British equivalent will make the point better than any number of words, and only in France will you find a newspaper strip cartoon starring a goat cheese with a supporting cast of chestnuts. Honestly, I'm not making it up.

Good food eaten at a leisurely pace is an aspect of French life that is under threat from the modern mania for speed. Traditional French restaurants saw their business go down 15% even before the economic crash. Diners in a hurry are cutting down on the sacred menu, which traditionally has four or five courses. They are sharing plates, leaving out aperitifs and wine, and generally acting like apprentice Puritans. President Sarkozy was partly responsible for this, with his campaign against long lunch hours and his apparent ambition to make leisurely France into hyperactive America.

It has been reported by those who know that, in restaurant kitchens, culinary standards are slipping too. Chefs are under pressure to cut corners, and even the prestige of the chef is declining. Fast food has made its awful mark, seducing especially the young. In *Place de la République*, close to our apartment, the great central statue that symbolizes French liberty, gazed out directly at McDonald's, Kentucky Fried Chicken, and Buffalo Grill, with the Holiday Inn just behind her flowing skirts. There *seems* to be no doubt about who's winning this culture war.

But, as the travel writers like to say, there are still secret gems to be found among the thirteen thousand restaurants of Paris. They don't stay secret for long, or gems for that matter once their names have been published. Our "discovery" was a tiny bistro located in a dark back street and consisting of just ten plain wood tables inside a wine store with a traditional not-quite-vegetarian menu of things like tripe, pig's cheek and blood sausage. The young proprietor chose our inexpensive wine and described it with great ceremony. There were posters with clever French puns, which it took us most of dinner to figure out. The place was packed with boisterous young people, wearing scarves and coats against the chill of the room. We were the oldest people in the place by a margin of thirty or forty years. So all is not lost. Young people in France still love traditional food when they can find it. I would tell you the name and address of our undiscovered local bistro, but if anyone else "discovers" it, there won't be room for us.

Chapter 9

Charity Begins Chez Nous

*L*iving in Paris we learned a lot about garbage. You escape this knowledge when you stay in a hotel, but having an apartment meant that we had to conform to a whole ritual of disposal and recycling. Each apartment block had a set of strict rules about the separation of garbage categories, pick up dates, and so on. The sound track of our lives was the crash of bottles being dropped into the glass container, and the big bins rumbling out to the curb to meet their carefully scheduled date with destiny, and then rumbling back again.

We owe all this sanitary activity to a famous Frenchman, Monsieur Eugène-René Poubelle who, in 1870, became Prefect of Paris. His self-appointed mission was to clean up the filthy city, which he achieved in 1884 by requiring every household to have a special container for garbage, which was then emptied at regular intervals by carts that traveled around the city, announcing their arrival by blasts on a hunting horn. *Et voila*, Paris was cleaned up, and M.Poubelle became a kind of hero. To this very day the noble garbage can is known, in French, as *la poubelle*. There's fame for you.

All this is very fine and should make us feel good, except that when the big garbage bins were rolled out to the street poor and homeless people appeared from nowhere and started digging in the garbage for any usable or edible items it might contain. This is not what we wanted to see in one of the most expensive cities in the world.

In December the spirit of charity should be active, even if it lies dormant from January to November. There are a lot of poor and homeless people in Paris. In January, a couple of blocks from where we were staying, hundreds of middle class Parisians moved into tents along the Canal Saint-Martin as a protest in support of the homeless. There are plans to do the same every year.

Paris was full of pathetic beggars, many of them old women, squatting in doorways or on the cold pavements. You couldn't get on the Metro without being serenaded by a beggar of the musical kind. The street musicians of Paris have gone downhill in recent years. Sometimes you would hear a really talented violinist or saxophone player, obviously trained at the *conservatoire*. But many had nothing more than a portable CD player, or a Karaoke machine. But there they were, it seemed in every subway car, in your face with their paper cup and their sad cry for help.

Guilt: it's hard to escape it. In hard times we should be twice as charitable. But if I had given one Euro coin to every beggar and street musician I encountered on a typical day it would have added up to at least twenty Euros (say $25), or more than a hundred and fifty dollars a week not counting Sundays, which was beyond my charitable budget. On the other hand my wife and I spent thirty four Euros on two cups of coffee and two slices of apple tart in a café near *L'Opèra*: guilt.

The tourists and the more affluent citizens of Paris didn't seem to notice the recession. The streets around the famous stores were almost too crowded to move. The most expensive hotels and restaurants were full. Guilt, like its great interpreter Sigmund Freud, is not fashionable in *haute bouregoise* France, it's not chic, and to be unfashionable is to be invisible. The poor are always with us, but they have no style, which in this most stylish of cities, is the ultimate misfortune.

Chapter 10

On Your Bike

My guidebook said: "Riding a bicycle in Paris is extremely dangerous," which should surely rate high on any list of statements of the obvious. But it was such a discouraging and dogmatic statement that I decided to test it. There was no need to buy a bike because Paris is one of several European cities that have provided free (or almost free) bicycles on a grand scale: they're called VelLib, and you see them everywhere. People use them to commute to work or college, and whole families use them for Sunday outings.

These free bikes are a marvelous idea. You may need a bike only for a limited time, or to go from A to B and not back. Or the weather may be fine in the morning, and rain in the afternoon. You just take any one of 20,000 bikes from any one of the almost a thousand stations around the city, and return it wherever you like. It's the perfect solution for getting around in Paris, provided your life insurance is up to date.

They say that you never forget how to ride a bike, but I've forgotten so many things in my life that it seemed more than probable that I had forgotten this one. Nevertheless I decided to give it a try, got my subscription card, and launched out with a bicycle from the stand outside our apartment. It took me a while to get started. Some schoolgirls on break came out into the street to smoke and to watch my fumbling efforts to get on the move. I chose a likely looking bike, pulled it out of the rack, and prepared to set off. I didn't get far because the bike had no chain. The second one I tried wouldn't come out of its electronic rack at all, but the third one did. Under the skeptical gaze of the schoolgirls I adjusted the saddle, put my briefcase in the basket, and pushed off. Miracle of miracles I could still ride a bike, and even keep it on a fairly straight course. The wisdom of the body is more durable than the wisdom of the mind.

Pedaling around some quiet local streets for practice I decided that my VelLib was a very nice bicycle indeed: smooth riding, even over the cobbles, with a simple three speed gear change and excellent brakes. Each bike came with a lock, a basket, a bell, and a bright warning light in front. There were no helmets, but safety advice was right in front of the rider, on the handlebar, couched in the first person reflexive imperative: "I will obey stop signs; I will not ride on the sidewalks; I will not go the wrong way down one-way streets". All these rules were widely ignored.

The VelLib may not be the right machine for the Tour de France but it was the best town bike I've ever ridden. So many people love these bicycles that they have been vanishing at a great rate, some of them turning up for sale in Africa. Almost half the original bikes have been stolen, and vandalism is a huge problem, which is a depressing commentary on human (or at least young male human) nature.

But my bike was in fine shape, even if the rider was not. As the old reflexes crept back I ventured out on to the main boulevards which, in spite of the bike lanes, were rather scary. I wish I had tried this in summer rather than mid-winter, and when my knees were twenty years younger. But I became an enthusiastic VelLib user, at least on sunny days. I was never able to match the skill of the locals at weaving through the insane traffic with one hand on the handlebar and a cell phone in the other. But I picked up speed, and adopted the necessary fatalistic attitude. The guide book was right: cycling in Paris *is* extremely dangerous. But it is the ecologically correct way to go, even if it kills you.

Chapter II

An Invisible History

*P*aris, like all ancient cities, is full of ghosts – not those supernatural spirits in white sheets that haunt the imaginations of silly people, but ghosts in the profounder sense of real traces from the real past. A city like Paris has ghosts on every corner. Walking the streets of Montparnasse or Montmartre you can sit in cafés where Molière, Hemingway and Toulouse Lautrec actually sat. You can see the homes of Delacroix and Corot, and the night club where Eric Satie played, and of course the great palaces that housed the long running soap opera of the *ancien régime*. And just down the road from our apartment was the Bastille where the revolution of 1789 began.

We have to go a bit further back to find the ghosts that interest me, all the way to the eighteenth century, when men like Voltaire, Rousseau, Diderot, Montesquieu, d'Alembert, and indeed Benjamin Franklin, held court in the salons and coffee houses. The Café Procope in Saint Germain was a favorite gathering place. Paris was (to use the modern idiom) ground zero for the intellectual revolution called The Enlightenment (in French *l'éclairage*, literally "lighting up.") It's not too much to say that the foundations of the modern world were laid right here.

Paris in the 1700s was not in any way "modern." If we could be transported there we would find it barbaric. The unpopular kings Louis XV and XVI remained skulking out at Versailles with their corrupt courts, the city was filthy and racked with disease and violence, and you can forget about equality or human rights. But under cover of the city's chaos, like mushrooms under a heap of manure, a few men were cultivating transformative ideas. Some of these ideas made it into America's Declaration of Independence: Life, Liberty, the Pursuit of Happiness, and the right of the people to alter or abolish any government that became destructive of these goals - dangerous stuff then and now

The men playing with these reckless thoughts were given the collective name *Les Philosophes*. This label distinguishes them from modern academic philosophers, who just create theories about the world within a rigid framework of orthodoxy. *Les Philosophes* were wildly original and actively engaged in politics and public debate. Many of them suffered for it, but they were celebrities in their time. It is hard to believe that intellectuals were once admired and almost worshipped, much the way media and sports celebrities are today.

There was no single Enlightenment movement or ideology. In Scotland and Britain it took a different direction. There was less faith in the power of reason and more focus on irrational sentiments like self-love and tribalism. But the important point is that there was an intense and continuous debate about fundamental questions: the best form of government, the rights of the individual, the definition of human nature, and so on, explosive questions that modern academics scarcely dare to touch.

I have been a casual student of these eighteenth century debates over the years, and I believe that they have important things to tell us in the twenty first century.*Without writing a thesis, which nobody would read, I will boldly summarize some of the main threads of French Enlightenment thought.

- The only way we can plan the future is by knowing and understanding the past.
- We can only think clearly and plan rationally if we first abandon the search for all kinds of gods, down to and including the worship of technologies, national flags, and celebrities.
- A rational man must question all habits and traditions, and reject all supernatural explanations.
- Knowledge, not faith or tradition, is the key to a better future.
- English and Scottish philosophers remind us that technological and scientific progress is not the same as moral or social progress, and may be its opposite.
- Education is the most important thing a society does.

Les Philosophes of Paris have been dead for more than two hundred years. But through their writings they still speak to us about the human condition more clearly and directly than most of our modern commentators.

"As long as people believe in absurdities they will continue to commit atrocities."
Voltaire

"There is no crueler tyranny than that which is perpetuated under the shield of law and in the name of justice."
Charles de Montesquieu

"We are born weak, we need strength; helpless, we need aid; foolish, we need reason. All that we lack at birth, all that we need when we come to man's estate, is the gift of education."
Jean-Jacques Rousseau

"Watch out for the fellow who talks about putting things in order! Putting things in order always means getting other people under your control."
Denis Diderot

"High office, is like a pyramid; only two kinds of animals reach the summit--reptiles and eagles."
Jean d'Alembert

Note: There are many books that will tell you much more about this fascinating period of history, including Neil Postman's, *Building a Bridge to the Eighteenth Century* (1999), and *The Encyclopaeda of the Enlightenment* by Alan Charles Kors (2002) (four volumes, very expensive, so get it from the library!)

Chapter 12

Who Really Loves Paris?

*E*verybody claims to love Paris. They love it in the summer, when it sizzles, and even in the winter, when it drizzles, which it always does. But, after our last visit, I found myself in a minority of one. I didn't much love Paris any more.

This is not the city's fault. It is still one of the most beautiful in the world. The streets and buildings are probably authentic, although one can never be quite sure. But no city in history had been as over-praised, over-romanticized, and over-sold as Paris. Rome had pretensions, in the great days of the Caesars, ancient Athens is reputed to have been quite a fine city to visit, although you wouldn't want to live there, and modern New York is famous for its grandstanding claims to be the world's greatest city. But, when it comes to hype and hyperbole, no place compares to Paris.

Paris is the single most popular tourist destination on the planet, hosting an estimated seventy million French and foreign visitors every year. Six million of them find it necessary to climb the Eiffel Tower. Jumbo jets full of Japanese, Americans and Australians come roaring into Charles de Gaulle airport every few minutes. Since the Channel Tunnel was built, the British have spearheaded the biggest invasion since the Hundred Years War. Fast European express trains bring more tourists in from everywhere. It is even rumored that a few brave souls have *driven* to Paris, although they were never heard from again.

This tells the visitor what to expect. Paris not a primarily French experience, or a cultural experience, or even a romantic experience: it is an international tourist experience. Even in mid-winter the sidewalks are blocked by gawping sightseers, clutching maps and bottles of spring water, the restaurants resound with the twanging accents of Manchester, Milwaukee or Melbourne, and every major exhibition or show attracts a line of foreigners that stretches around the block.

Travel agents could help to rationalize mass tourism by exercising a little discretion at the point of sale. A few simple questions such as: "Do you like to stand in line for five hours to see a lot of very large, very dark religious paintings by artists who died four hundred years ago, or do you prefer to play Blackjack?" would help to distinguish the people who would enjoy Paris from those who would have a better time in Las Vegas. But, like all brilliantly simple solutions, this one will never be implemented. Only Robespierre could solve the problem of tourists in Paris.

The Parisians themselves are almost invisible. In fact, they are moving out of the city as fast as they can. In a poll taken in *La Parisienne* magazine revealed that six out of ten Parisians want to leave the place entirely. They are moving to smaller cities and country towns with less crowding, less traffic, fewer tourists, less outrageous property prices, and above all less crime. Those who must keep jobs in Paris are commuting up to two hundred miles on high-speed trains, just so they don't have to live there.

Here is a case where Monsieur Disney and his team of clever illusionists could actually do some good. Euro Disney is already flourishing just outside Paris. Why not return the compliment, and build a Parisian theme park in America? Disney's magicians-in-plastic could reproduce Paris in some convenient empty location, perhaps in Kansas. They could sell cheap flights and a single bargain-price ticket to cover all the attractions, including a fake Eiffel Tower, a fake Louvre with a fake Mona Lisa, a fake Metro without the beggars, and a fake French dinner at a fake Arpège. They could also provide plenty of public bathrooms. The real Paris would become a delightful city again, and the real Parisians could come out of hiding and live there.

It's always a shame when cities or even villages are depopulated just because they are so popular. Too many tourists make any place unlivable. Then, by definition, it becomes nothing but a historic monument. Take Stonehenge, for example, or Machu Pichu, where the locals were driven out by hordes of visitors centuries ago.

That is the sad fate of Paris today. It has become a theme park, a monument to what it used to be. I'm never going there again, or at least not until our trip in the spring. We wouldn't want to miss Paris in the spring.

Prologue To Part Ii
Paris Is Not France

"We have come five hundred miles by rail through the heart of France. What a bewitching land it is! What a garden!"
MARK TWAIN, *THE INNOCENTS ABROAD*

For many years tourism in France was limited to a few well-known destinations: Paris, the Chateaux of the Loire, the Alps, the Dordogne, and fashionable places along the Riviera. There were good reasons for this. Well into the twentieth century the roads were in poor condition, the rail system was limited, and the French heartland was not a place where anyone would want to go. They call it "The Real France" or *"La France profonde,"* and you can learn what it was really like from an eye-opening book by historian Graham Robb called *The Discovery of France* (2007).

Robb was dissatisfied with the history he got from books, and cycled 14,000 miles through the heart of France talking to people and collecting their memories. This book totally changed my image of France. The best comparison for English social history would be Ronald Blythe's *Akenfield*, and for America (but less seriously) Bill Bryson's *The Lost Continent*.

> *"Just over a hundred years ago French was a foreign language to the majority of the population. It was a country that still had not been mapped in its entirety. A little further back in time sober accounts described a land of ancient tribal divisions, prehistoric communication networks, and pre-Christian beliefs."*

Every nation becomes a different world once you leave the metropolis. The region of Languedoc, where we have our second home, lagged behind the rest of France because of its remoteness. On the eve of the French Revolution it would have taken two or three weeks to travel there from Paris. Episodes of religious persecution of Protestants in Languedoc from the 1500s to the 1700s created a sense of separateness, as did the language. In the late 1800s it is estimated that 80-90% of the communes in the Languedoc were non-French speaking. The common language was Occitan, a Latin-derived language that still lingers on in the accents and vocabulary of the region, much to the confusion of those of us who try to communicate in standard French.

Robb describes an almost-wild land, criss-crossed by millions of livestock in the great *transhumance* of spring and autumn, a land where most women went barefoot and map makers sent out from Paris were persecuted and sometimes killed. By the late-1800s the map of post roads and railways in Languedoc was still virtually a blank.

This is very different from what tourists find there today. But we have lived in two ancient villages in Languedoc – Aniane and Saint Quentin la Poterie – and both are full of reminders of the past. The old stone houses, narrow streets and archaic accents could come right out of the nineteenth century, and some old postcards of "our" village taken in the 1890s show another world entirely, a world of marginal agriculture, brutal hard work, and poverty.

The following essays are about these villages as they are now, and indirectly about the impact of modernity and tourism on the ancient culture of the French countryside.

Chapter 13

Peter Mayle and the Anglo Invasion

It seems that everyone dreams about spending a year in rural France. This is the fault of Peter Mayle, whose charming and enormously successful 1989 book *A Year in Provence* told the story of his family's adventures moving into a house in a village in the south. It sounded idyllic and wonderful although, soon after he published *A Year in Provence*, Mayle moved to the even more idyllic and wonderful territory of Long Island.

Since Peter Mayle hit the publishing jackpot, there has been a deluge of books based on the same romantic dream – *A Year in Burgundy*, *A Year in Tuscany*, and so on. These stories have many similarities. The setting is invariably picturesque. The voluntary exiles buy an old farmhouse or château, and go through a painful period of restoration and decoration. They have trouble with the plumbing, the servants, the quaint locals, and the swimming pool. They spend millions of dollars, but it is worth it in the end.

I love reading these books. They are pure travel pornography. Even before Peter Mayle came along my wife and I had made a habit of renting a cottage (or *gite*) in some more or less emote place each summer, so we already knew a little about real life in the real French countryside. In the early eighties we rented a small house in an unfashionable village called Rouaix in an unfashionable part of Provence.

In retrospect Rouaix was a dim and faraway echo of the pre-industrial France that Robb was writing about, and the absolute opposite of the kind of village described by Peter Mayle. This is a radio essay I wrote about it at the time.

Chapter 14

Let Sleeping Dogs Lie

*L*ocals say that God spent the first five days of creation making Provence. It sounds like boosterism, until you get here.

This corner of southern France, folded between the mountains and the Mediterranean, has all the conventional qualities of paradise. The climate is mild and sunny, the landscape is lush and rolling, like a medieval painter's vision of the Garden of Eden, and the food and wine are better than anything found in this world.

This is the Provence that millions of tourists (including about half the population of Paris) come every year to visit. We come for its sophisticated beauty, for the life and landscape that has been a magnet for hundreds of poets, writers and painters over the centuries, including Robert Louis Stevenson, Lawrence Durrell, Henry James, Georges Brassens, Alphonse Daudet, Van Gogh, Cézanne, Ezra Pound, Nancy Mitford, Stendahl, F. Scott Fitzgerald, Collette, Rudyard Kipling, Nathaniel Hawthorne, Petrarch, and last but not least the Marquis de Sade.

From where I sit in our little house among the vines high in the hills called *Les Auzieres*, I can just see the rooftops below of the closest outpost of French civilization, the village of Roaix.

Roaix has the air of a place surprised to find itself stranded in time, at some indeterminate date between 1600 and 1850. There are a few steep, narrow streets, where muddy hunting dogs sleep and scratch through the day. There is a half-derelict chateau perched on a rocky height, and an ancient, windowless church. This is Roaix - all of it.

For a more sophisticated version of French country life, we must drive six kilometres to the provincial town of Vaison.

Vaison has been a hangout for idlers and parasites for more than two thousand years. The Romans used to come here for rest and re-laxation in Julius Caesar's time, and they left behind some impressive ruins - hence the full name of the town, Vaison la Romaine, also known as the Pompeii of France. Vaison is one of those rare places that never has been anything but a retreat, an escape from modern life.

Daily life in Vaison is like a meal in one of its old-fashioned res-taurants - full of formal manners left over from another age. Every meeting, including those between children, requires a polite saluta-tion and a handshake. The greeting of intimates involves one, two, three or four kisses on alternate cheeks, according to the warmth of the relationship.

Formal manners and public rituals show a community at peace with itself. The French in general have enormous respect for the dig-nity of others, placing equality higher in their value system than any other western nation, including the United States. In a small town like Vaison, respect for the equality of individuals implies good man-ners to everyone. This in turn produces that rarest of things in the modern world, a safe and civilized urban area.

Vaison will not escape the twentieth century much longer. It's a refuge and a magnet for people like us precisely because it's a bit of an anachronism, a stage set for our performance of visiting a French country town. Having created a world we can barely tolerate, we want a piece of their civilized and urbane community. And so do many others.

Vaison is on the edge of becoming an international tourist attraction. When the tourist wave breaks, its character as a sleepy spa will be swept away in a single season. Vaison will become like Avignon or Nice: busy and rich, but as dead as colonial Williamsburg.

Good manners will be the first casualty. There is a critical mass of outsiders beyond which politeness must vanish. There are too many differences, too many misunderstandings, and too little mutual respect. Swamped by loud, mannerless strangers, the community will adapt. People will become more hurried and brusque, citizens of the great world, cosmopolitans.

At least the little village of Roaix is safe. Roaix is not a fantasy of French country life, it *is* French country life - far too smelly, dirty, petty and grim for any tourist to enjoy. No coach parties will come to Roaix with its shabby alleys, sneaking cats and battered dogs, its rotten flyblown ruins and permanently closed shops.

They will go to Vaison.

But it is not a happy thought that, when Vaison becomes just another tourist trap, it will be because of people like us: nice people, hordes of us, driving our rented cars through the villages, disturbing the sleeping dogs, claiming our moment of peace and civility in the pretty old country town, looking for a world we have irretrievably lost.

Chapter 15

Life in a French Village : First Year

*I*n the year 2000, just after the world had failed to end, we had an opportunity to spend a whole year in a French village house rented from a colleague, and we jumped at the chance. So we arrived in Aniane in the Herault Valley, twenty-five kilometers west of Montpellier.

Aniane had no superficial charm, but plenty of character. It was founded, according to legend, in the year 777 and survives as an almost-intact medieval village with about two thousand inhabitants and no parking space. There is no record of the earliest structures, but maps and sketches from five hundred years ago show the street pattern and many of the buildings virtually as they are now. It always gave us a thrill to imagine that people walked these same narrow streets five centuries ago, grumbling about the weather and the dogs, and speaking the ancient language of Occitan, as they still do.

Like any new immigrants, we arrived with many anxieties. How would we live here, so far from the familiar culture and comforts of Long Island? Would we be able to manage life's basic survival tasks like understanding the TV schedule, making friends with the neighborhood cats, and finding a bakery that had really good croissants? This is a good example of how we always worry about the wrong things. Croissants were not a problem: there was a bakery at each end of our street. The TV was so exceptionally bad that the schedule was irrelevant, and the local cats were more friendly than was strictly necessary.

We arrived in September, a month of changes in the south of France. The weather was still mostly beautiful, but showing ominous hints of the rainy, windy autumn just ahead. Virtually all the summer visitors were heading home. The roads were jammed with millions of French, German, British and Scandinavian sun worshippers, returning to their schools and their jobs, reluctantly abandoning this southern playground. The tourist season was over. From the Riviera to Provence, and even in our less fashionable region of Languedoc, there was an almost audible collective sigh of relief from the people who actually live down there year round.

They call this period the *arrière-saison* – literally the back of the season. It is a true autumn – economic, spiritual, meteorological, and biological. Most of the restaurants and tourist spots are still open at the beginning of September. But during the next few weeks they close one by one. Even the shops cut down on their opening hours, and the owners will retire to their winter homes in Spain, or former French Africa, or even in some cases Florida or Cuba. They'll be back in April.

Meanwhile, we had only just arrived. Our neighbors found this amazing, and almost perverse, like moving into your summer place in the Hamptons just after Labor Day. They were too polite to ask directly why we were there, why we had chosen to live in a village house, and what on earth we were going to do with ourselves through the winter.

We were asking the same questions. We knew that life in such a village would be different, but we hadn't quite realized *how* different. For example we had to get accustomed to a lot less personal space. When you have lived in the American suburbs for a while, you take it for granted that everyone has plenty of space. Wide streets, big sprawling houses, half-acre gardens, and double or quadruple garages seem entirely normal. A medieval village in the south of France was not the same.

Aniane was a maze of narrow streets, some of them scarcely more than alleyways. Our street, Rue de la Tour or street of the tower was exactly 180 centimeters or 71 inches wide – I measured it. It was just barely possible to drive a small car into the street. But as I discovered, much to the amusement of the neighbors, it was almost impossible to back it out again because of the tight turns. This guaranteed that there was virtually no motor traffic in the center of the village, and therefore no traffic noise. Parking was a nightmare or a challenge, depending on how you looked at it. After a few weeks of living there, my definition of a "parking space" became more and more elastic. I soon gave up the idea of finding a neat little box marked out by white lines. Any scrap of sidewalk without a cat sleeping on it was a parking space. The triangular corner behind the garbage cans beside the river was a parking space. The spot between the fountain and the church door was a parking space, if I was lucky enough to get it.

The fact that the village architecture discouraged motor vehicles had many advantages. When you can't drive up to your own front door, shopping is drastically limited. There was no point loading up the car at the supermarket in the next town, because every item has to be carried through a quarter of a mile of narrow streets. It was easier to use the village shops. Everything of importance was right on our doorstep: three bakers, a butcher, a farm shop, several wineries, two grocers, a drugstore, and a market every Thursday.

Miscellaneous purchases, like flashlight batteries and an ironing board, led us down a narrow alleyway to the amazing, un-advertised emporium of Monsieur Vidal. The cliché of Aladdin's Cave has been overworked, but in the case of Monsieur Vidal's store, no other cliché will do. He had everything, or he would get it for you next day – whether a bottle of barbecue lighting fluid or a packet of computer disks. Everybody came here, and the gnome-like Monsieur Vidal assisted by his slightly mad poodle Bruno orchestrated the shopping needs of the village like air traffic controllers at a busy airport. He also delivered bottled gas personally, which you will realize is no small matter when I tell you about the stairs. His opening and closing schedule was completely arbitrary, and unknown even to the locals. Customers would peer down the narrow alley to see if Vidal's battered car was there, or the plastic basket that he sometimes remembered to hang out as an "open" sign. If not, they would shrug and carry on.

The original builders of Aniane had no interest in wide boulevards for convenient shopping, but they did like to build *upwards* for security against invading Saracens, Moors, Spaniards and, more recently, tourists. In the old days, cattle lived on the lowest floor of the houses, and hay was kept in the attics to be dropped down to the animals through a shaft. The family lived on the middle two floors, presumably with bales of hay whizzing past their ears. Our house wasn't as wide as an American double garage, but it was four stories tall. The front door was three feet above the level of the street, and that was just the beginning. The rooms were high, and the stairs were steep. In the first few weeks, we spent a lot of time gasping for breath.

All this climbing had a health payoff. If we wanted this kind of workout in America we would have to buy one of those exercise machines called a Stairmaster. But we built leg muscles like Olympic athletes just by living in Aniane. Also, the ordinary temptations of daily life were much reduced. When you have your first *apéritif* on the top floor terrace, and the bottle is in the kitchen down two steep flights of stairs, you're likely to settle for just admiring the view.

We necessarily lived close to our neighbors on all sides. They were on top of us, and we were on top of them. There were no suburban open spaces to soften our togetherness. The walls of the houses were thick, and made of solid granite: but the windows were open. So we got to know people, through their family conversations and cooking smells, as well as by the inescapable encounters in the narrow street. It worked very well. Everyone kept their voices low, nobody played loud music, and the after-lunch siesta hour was more or less sacred.

Laundry was an important part of this public/private life. Very few village houses had indoor dryers, and not many had back yards. So the only place to hang your wet laundry was out the front window. This gave the streets a festive air on a sunny day, and created a harmless competition between the housewives (who still exist there) over the quantity, the quality and the frequency of their washing. Young widows could also use this public forum for a bit of discreet advertising – some surprisingly filmy garments were on display – and the presence or absence of hanging laundry was a very good indication of the day's weather. Abundant laundry meant that it would stay dry, and it would be a good day for a trip. The housewives were almost never wrong, and considerably more accurate than the official weather forecast.

The central social space in the village used to be the public washing tubs behind the chapel. Now that everyone has running water, the action has shifted to the hairdressing salon beside the town hall. My wife Diane and I both patronized this useful establishment, but we felt a bit conspicuous. The windows allowed every passer-by to look in, which they did, and many people came in for conversation, or to suggest hairstyle improvements to whoever happened to be in the chair at the time. These were usually on the lines of "More Henna," because flaming red hair was very much the fashion with women of all ages. Monsieur Vidal spent more time there than in his own general store up the street. Everyone knew that if Monsieur Vidal was dispensing coffee and gossip at the hairdresser's, his own shop must be closed. The general effect was of being in a fishbowl with a lot of friendly but unfamiliar fish.

As in any French village, there was an enormous amount of talk. Everyone seemed to know everyone else, and they held intense, loud and apparently continuous discussions in the street, the post office, the *tabac*, and the hairdressers. They had no need of cellular phones.

What they were saying was another matter. There was, to put it mildly, a regional accent. All languages have regional accents and, generally speaking, the farther south you travel the more incomprehensible the accent becomes. If you've been to the American deep south, you know what I mean. Britain is a rare exception to this rule, its most peculiar accents being found in the far north while proper English is spoken only in the south. But France is not an exception. The south is another country, they say things differently there.

This had me worried at first. My French is pretty bad, but I can usually manage an ordinary conversation. Here, standing in the market or the post office, I understood nothing. I might as well have been in Mississippi, or Scotland.

This linguistic incompetence was explained when I learned a little more about the history of the region. It is called Languedoc, which is a corruption of the phrase "Langue d'Oc," or language of Oc. Back in the early middle ages, this part of France spoke a unique language, Occitan, derived from Latin and completely different from the French spoken in the north. In fact the linguistic division was based on those who said "oc" for "oui" (southerners) and those who said something like "oïl" (northerners). Generations later it was clear to me that the old way of speech still survived in the south. These people weren't speaking French, they were speaking Oc. No wonder I couldn't understand them. I always had trouble with Latin at school, and finally dropped out of the class after a long series of Fs and a score of ten percent in the final examination.

Whatever they were saying, the people of Aniane were bound together by more than physical closeness. They had a strong common identity as "Anianais," just as the people in the next village of Gignac saw themselves as "Ginacois." This feeling of community was constantly reinforced by common activities. Although the village had only 2,000 inhabitants and you could walk across it in five minutes, there was always something going on - free concerts, poetry readings, pétanque matches – something for everybody. It was all orchestrated from the eighteenth century town hall right in the center of the village where the mayor presided more like a tribal leader than a politician.

Public spaces were intensively used. The sports field was claimed by the circus, and for outdoor concerts. The Place des Penitents in the center of the village hosted flea markets, fish stalls, outdoor dinners, brass bands and art shows. The Post Office car park was taken over for a motorcycle show, a country fair, a midsummer celebration, and more music. The theater in the old monastery put on regular plays, some of them classics, and the village hall was the venue for Lotto, agricultural events, and live pop music concerts. The twelfth century Chapel of the Penitents had a new art show every month, and the Catholic church of Saint Sauveur hosted some splendid classical music concerts. We might almost have been in a big city rather than in a very small village. The community activities wore us out.

There were a surprising number of formal and informal groups. Old men who hung out at the Esplanade café, young people who hung out at the opposite end of the village, in the PMU bar, several political parties, the wine growers' association, the Club of the Third Age, a theater group, and an organization called *Vivre à Aniane*. The latter was made up of middle-aged people, ironically known as *soixante huitards* (sixty eighters) – referring to the wave of youth revolts in France in 1968 that receded and left these fiftysomethings beached in places like Aniane. They worked against the odds to bring more liberal and modern attitudes to the village.

Public benches were everywhere. The *banc publique* is a French institution, and the popular singer George Brassens wrote a famous love song about it. People actually used these benches, not so much for romantic encounters as for gossiping and quiet sitting. This is not a negligible part of village public life. You'd have to walk a long way in most American towns to find a public bench other than in a park. The idea that a fit and healthy person might want to just stop and sit and think for a while is alien to us.

A great deal of the community's life remained obscure to us because of language problems and a natural reluctance on the part of the villagers to explain themselves to outsiders. Why should they? We grew accustomed to the twenty-four hour chimes from the clock tower close by, the idiosyncratic opening hours of the local shops, the ubiquitous cats, the impossible parking, and the cranky heating system in our rented house. We made friends, many of them feline, and we have returned to Aniane many times. It was and is a mirror image of Peter Mayle's portrait of a village in the South of France, but it gave us a taste of what life there could be like. Ten years later we were back, searching for a new home in a new village.

Chapter 16

The Ideal Village

*H*ow do you find your ideal village? For years my wife and I have been auditioning villages in France in search of the perfect vacation hideaway and eventual retirement retreat, if retirement still exists by the time we get to it. This has been an unsystematic search, depending very much on vague inspirations and random discoveries. Truly organized people would have a map of Europe marked up in grid squares, and a list of desirable features like those they use to create league tables of The Best Places to Live or The Best Places to Retire. But on closer inspection these turn out to be not exactly the "best" places but rather the safest places, where retirees will be surrounded with walls and gates, hospitals and nursing homes, and people exactly like themselves.

Our search has been more like a dating game than a rational decision-making process. Episodes of love at first sight were followed by indifference at second sight, sudden infatuations led to equally sudden disappointments. Also, like the search for an ideal partner the search for an ideal village is expensive and exhausting. Common sense says that nothing in real life is ideal, which is why we have two separate words to describe the way things are and the way we'd like them to be. But it does no harm to try.

We visited a long lost cousin of mine who lives with his wife in a beautiful spot in the Loire Valley, in France, with very little other company apart from some donkeys, some sheep, two dogs and a whole lot of cats. Heredity must count for something. There wasn't a strip mall or a housing development anywhere in sight. It seemed to us an impossibly isolated place. But the fact is that my cousin, in his remote house, knows all about his not-very-near neighbors, their families, and their life histories. In the closely-packed suburbs of Long Island we scarcely know any of our neighbors. They might as well be on another planet.

There has to be a middle way between the seclusion of the deep countryside and the blank anonymity of the suburbs and there is: the village. I love villages: looking at them, and reading about them, and living in them. Some of the villages I've been lucky enough to call home have been absolute gems: beautiful to look at, convenient, and above all friendly. There's an urban myth that you won't be accepted in a village until your family has lived there for three or four generations, but that's a hundred years out of date. Most villages these days are full of immigrants and "strangers," and a new resident is always an object of curious, usually friendly interest. Villagers need something to talk about.

Another myth is that there's no privacy in a village, and everybody knows your business. But, once you close your front door, you can have exactly as much privacy as you could have anywhere else. Neighbors may observe your comings and goings, and take note of your visitors, but nosy neighbors are as common in London or Los Angeles as they are in any village. You can have privacy in a village, but not anonymity, and that's good because most antisocial behavior depends on anonymity. It's not true, as many readers of Agatha Christie's Miss Marple books may assume, that any picturesque village is a war zone with a murder every week. Villages are not without crime, but they are much safer than towns or cities. Once, when I was living in a lovely village in Suffolk, England, the local vet was murdered in mysterious circumstances. But that sort of thing is not as common as Public Television would have us believe, and in any case the locals soon figured out who did it, and why. They just didn't care to mention the fact to the police

Mysterious murders apart, a village is comforting because you know the whole place and most of the people. It's typically quiet, because the local teenagers escape as soon as they can to create havoc elsewhere. Quiet is worth a lot these days. A village gives instant access to the surrounding countryside. With any luck there are no shops, other than the essential food and wine shops, and therefore no temptation to go shopping.

Urban dwellers always complain that a village can't have great art galleries, theaters, or symphony orchestras, which is true. But they can have something better: real artists, real actors, and real musicians, who are creators rather than consumers of culture. There is nothing more satisfying than a nice amateur village performance or exhibition. It makes us feel that we ourselves may not be hopelessly without talent, and that we can be creative too.

In our search for the ideal village there were practical geographical choices to be made: did we want to live in trendy Provence or the less spectacular, less touristy region of the Languedoc to the west? The showcase villages of Provence with their four- star restaurants and glittering boutiques are absolutely beautiful, but too much like eating *foie gras* every day. In the season they are packed with people talking loudly in many languages and threatening to flatten our tiny Peugot with their huge brand new SUVs. A sense of class inferiority can be salutary for a week or two, but we don't want to live with it. Languedoc was the place for us, so we headed in that direction. West of the Rhone the antique shops slowly give way to junk shops selling much the same stuff, property prices drop by a third and modest restaurants serve good, honest local wine, the kind that takes the enamel off your teeth.

Having arrived at a certain age we were wary of those spectacular hill villages that dot the southern landscape, because even a slight disability could make them unlivable. On the other hand the threat of global warming made us think twice about settling in some picturesque river valley. This is no time to become amphibious. Naturally we wanted a place with all the basic shops, services, and restaurants, so life doesn't have to depend entirely on the motor car.

A living village also needs to be *doing* something. If Aniane was a village dominated by politics and wine, Saint Quentin la Poterie is a village dominated by art, particularly pottery. It has been so for at least five hundred years, because of the excellent local clay. A lot of ceramic artists have been attracted here, so now there at least twenty-five active potteries around the village, and people come here from all over Europe just to buy pottery. The result is that Saint Quentin is cosmopolitan and easier for foreigners to integrate into, but still essentially French. So, ten years after leaving Aniane, we found ourselves buying a small, ancient house in Saint Quentin la Poterie

This fondness of mine for villages is ridiculously nostalgic I know, and quite unrealistic, like a taste for steam trains. But I'm not going to give it up. As Miss Marple pointed out, a village is a microcosm of the world, with all of human nature in it, including the essential village idiot. That, I hope, is where I will fit in.

Chapter 17

The Idea of The South

When we say "The South" we usually mean the group of red states below the Mason Dixon Line that share a particular history and culture. In Europe "The South" is also a term that carries more than its simple geographical meaning. In the European imagination "The South" is a fantasy land, rather like California or Florida or Hawaii in the American imagination, a place where you can escape and enjoy the good life. In the Northeastern United States we get a tantalizing hint of the The South every summer when the temperature rises, and the pools are opened. But it doesn't last long, and it doesn't bring with it the whole landscape and lifestyle that make up the year-round southern dream. Even as we stand sweating at the barbecue, we know what's coming next.

The gravitational pull of The South is familiar to anyone who grew up in a gray, chilly northern climate. When I was a kid it was a ritual for our family to travel sixty miles to the south coast of England for our summer vacation, because the rain was a couple of degrees warmer there. Millions of optimists join the annual southward trek, some only as far as the south shore of Long Island, but others adventuring all the way to Costa Rica, or Greece, or Morocco, or the South of France. In a couple of weeks almost the whole population of Northern Europe, and quite a few Americans too will be on the move, all in the same direction.

The South is romantic territory - think of the music, the poetry, the love stories, and the sun-drenched movies that are set there. Picasso and Matisse were drawn by the southern light, composers like Mendelssohn and Tchaikovsky offered lyrical tributes to Spain and Italy, Shakespeare put his doomed young lovers in Verona, not London, and of course just about every celebrity in the past two centuries has taken up residence in The South at one time or another. Right now you might encounter Angelina Jolie, Brad Pitt, or Johnny Depp for example. Even I have heard of them. The southern scenery is so familiar that we feel we have been there even if we haven't: the cypresses and palms, lovely stone houses, the blue ocean and exotic flowers, the animated outdoor cafes and festivals. It's all there, and it's all real.

Yet the romance of The South goes only so far. Once we pass the Tropic of Cancer we arrive in the equatorial zone that contains some of the most turbulent and violent places in the world. Here the southward migration goes into reverse. Everyone who can is doing their best to move north in search of security and freedom, but that's another story.

The regular inhabitants of The South see its golden reputation mainly as a way of attracting tourists, and just get on with their ordinary lives as if they were living in Kansas. But northerners can't get enough of it, at least for a short time. They arrive at the beginning of summer full of joyful anticipation. But within a few days they begin complaining about the heat, the biting bugs, the prices, the food, and the fact that nothing happens quickly enough. Then they go home to tell their friends and neighbors what a splendid time they had down there, in The South. That's the nature of paradise, I suppose. It's a wonderful place to visit, but only the most decadent and self-indulgent people would want to actually live here.

Chapter 18

Not Quite a Stranger

*E*very summer we find ourselves once again in a familiar corner of
the South of France. I love that phrase "We find ourselves." It's a
wonderfully old-fashioned formula that seems to suggest a happy accident without intentionality, desire, planning, or expense.

But, however we excuse it, here we are again. How remarkable it
is that one can jump from one world to another literally overnight,
and that we can communicate with the world just as easily from a
French village as we can from Long Island. The age of miracles has
not passed. It has only just begun.

There is always something awkward about these arrivals and departures. The village doesn't appear and vanish at our convenience
like Brigadoon. It stays stolidly in place all the time, and has done
since the fourteenth century. We are the ones who appear and vanish,
picking up village life for a few weeks or months and then leaving the
real inhabitants (the Saint Quentinois as they call themselves) to get
on with it.

This is not so very unusual. There are parts of Florida, for example, where an elderly population washes in and out on a tide of
temperature, moving a thousand miles and fifteen degrees of latitude

twice a year so they need never be cold or hot. College towns have similar transient populations, as do tourist spots everywhere. Coming and going is a very human activity. But those who come and go usually have a definite reason, which is clearly understood by those who stay.

Here in France we are not exactly tourists or students, and we are certainly not climate refugees. The village may be "south" in European terms but in fact is at about the same latitude as Boston. This is not a sub-tropical paradise.

So our arrival here is never easy to explain, even to ourselves. It's hard to know what kind of welcome we can expect, or deserve. Not surprisingly we are recognized and cordially greeted by the butcher, baker, the general store manager, the post office clerk, the restaurant owner, the local cats, and especially by Pascal the do-it-all-handyman, to whom we owe a fistful of Euros for repairs done while we were away. He is especially glad to see us. The neighbors always seem friendly, although they invariably ask how long we are planning to stay *this* time. At least we are not just summer people, and we get some credit for having survived in the village during two bitterly cold winters.

We are, I suppose, trying to establish a beachhead in this place, not a beachhead as a prelude to an invasion, but more as a down payment on a parallel life. Everyone needs a parallel life: it ought to be written into the Constitution. But we don't want to feel like invaders. One or two villages near here, and many more in fashionable Provence, have been totally taken over by second home owners and vacation renters, and are about as authentically French as Euro Disney. Most of the year they are ghost towns that have to be guarded against burglars by special police patrols. Foreigners like us who come and go must make an extra effort to fit in. So we try to speak the language, shop in the village, join in local activities like flea markets, music festivals, and so on. Otherwise we will be dismissed as just another pair of barbarian invaders, another nail in the coffin of real village life.

So far so good. We will never be French, but perhaps we can create these French Avatars, who will live their parallel lives here, between the Cévennes Mountains and the Mediterranean Sea. Florida may be a kinder, gentler place, and better for the arthritis. But Florida will have to wait.

Chapter 19

A Visit to the Middle Ages

*O*ur nearest town is Uzès, four kilometers away, which has a fine historic center with a real castle. As we walked through the streets, looking for a place for lunch, we spotted a group of people dressed in medieval costumes, and carrying ancient musical instruments. This was irresistible. We followed them down the street, through a stone archway, and into a square that was like a stage set for a King Arthur movie. Not only were most of the buildings at least five hundred years old, but also the square was packed with people in medieval costume.

We stopped at an outdoor café thinking that, if this was some curious illusion, a bottle of the local wine might help it along. Our waiter, a cheerful young squire wearing a royal tabard, told us that this was indeed the once a year medieval festival of Uzès. We had just missed the festival of garlic the week before, but he assured us that this was better.

It was. For this one day the whole town had traveled back in time to the fourteenth century, when it was the first Royal Dukedom of France. The modern inhabitants of Uzès had transformed themselves, with beautifully realistic costumes, into lords and ladies, priests and monks, nuns and jugglers, knights and squires, strolling musicians, and all the other characters familiar to the readers of medieval romances. The dark side was not forgotten: there were some nasty looking beggars, a truly hideous leper, a sinister wizard right our of Harry Potter, and plenty of poor artisans plying their various trades. Horses were tethered along the edge of the square, adding authentic sounds and smells.

The medieval band played their authentic instruments – heavy on the drums – and the dancers danced in spite of the temperature, which was around ninety degrees. The entertainers were correctly dressed in rags. Five hundred years ago entertainers were regarded as the lowest form of life. Today, for some inexplicable reason, they are treated like minor gods or fallen angels.

Children and even babies wore sixteenth century costumes, and were encouraged to play ancient games with hoops and spinning tops. The historical illusion was not complete, of course – there were plenty of funny anachronisms. Nikes could be seen peeking out from under some robes, the waiter at the adjoining restaurant, although dressed as a pious monk, was no better an example of Christian charity and forgiveness than any regular French waiter, and I saw a fire eater put down his flaming torches in order to answer his cell phone. Cigarettes and designer handbags were in evidence, half a millennium ahead of their time. But in general it was a fascinating show, street theater in its most comprehensive form. Everyone was a performer, and everyone was a spectator.

A few weeks before I had broadcast a radio essay in which I had talked about historical re-enactments, and I posed the rhetorical question: "Why are these events always about wars, like the Civil

War, and never about peace?" Well, here was my answer: the citizens of Uzès *were* re-enacting peace in the form of a market day – an innocent day of trade and sociability and entertainment – no blood, no death, no heroism, just fun. What could be more civilized than that?

Chapter 20

The Car of My Dreams

F rench drivers love their cars as much as Americans do, and maybe more. Driving is an essential part of the French experience and, if you don't worry too much about your own survival, a great pleasure too. This means that we must have a car in France, which in turn means that every time we go there we pay a small fortune to a rental company.

So we decided to buy our own vehicle. But we have a problem about where to keep it. The village, laid out some seven hundred years ago, was never designed for parking. There is a sort of garage under the house, a vaulted stone space where animals were kept in the old days. But the entrance is narrow, and so is the street: only a very small car can get in. After several experiments with borrowed cars, which greatly entertained the neighbors, we had the essential information. The very, very tiny Citroen C1 belonging to the baker would fit. A car larger than this by more than two centimeters in any dimension would not fit.

So we were in the market for a very small, very old, very cheap car. If you know anything at all about cars you know that this is not a good combination of requirements. Small cars tend to be more flimsily constructed than larger models, and they wear out faster. The owners of small cars are usually not rich, and so may be tempted to skimp on the maintenance until the vehicle begins to show signs of trouble and some idiotic foreigner can be persuaded to buy it.

We entered the French used car market in a suspicious mood: *caveat emptor*. We had no intention of falling for some fanciful tale about an old lady who used this car only once a week to drive to the Catholic Church. For one thing the Catholic Church is at the top of a steep hill, the kind of hill that chews up clutches, brakes, and gearboxes. For another, old ladies in France all seem to have the repressed desire to be Formula One drivers.

At least there were plenty of small cars to choose from. For the past half century the French automobile industry has been producing mainly compacts, partly because of the outrageous price of gasoline, and partly because the towns and villages are full of narrow streets with limited parking space. People with big egos do buy big cars to impress their neighbors, but they can never find a place to park and have to keep moving, like the Flying Dutchman. The most popular models are, by American standards, not much more than motorized skate boards, and are colloquially called *bagnoles* or old bangers..

The first step in French car buying, we discovered, was to watch the traffic. Cars for sale carry signs in their windows advertising the fact. You can run after them and speak to the owner when they park, or stop at a stop sign, not than anybody does stop at stop signs. My wife became very good at chasing down likely-looking vehicles and interrogating their owners. She had an amazing turn of speed, which most of these cars did not.

In the first week we had narrowed down our search to half a dozen makes and bottom-of-the-line models, none of them longer that 340 cm or wider than 150. Forget about color and style. We cruised around the local car dealers, learning a lot of arcane automotive vocabulary in the process, and shaking some greasy hands. One of the nice things about French car dealers was their indifference. You could wander about in the lot or showroom for as long as you liked without being bothered with sales talk. Even if you did find a sales person, he or she would just answer questions and then leave you alone. It could make car buying almost a pleasure.

But these tiny cars didn't inspire much confidence and, frankly, neither did the people selling them. We're waiting for that magic moment that happens in every French romantic film, when suddenly across a crowded car lot you see the one you love, and she is exactly the right size.

Chapter 21

Resident Aliens

*O*ut in the countryside beyond the village, away from the glow of street lights or any lights at all, the stars shine very bright. Looking up at nature's planetarium it is tempting to indulge in science fiction fantasies about other worlds and other lives out there.

There has been a flurry of interest in space aliens in France recently. Many unidentified flying objects have been spotted here over the years, and a new official French enquiry was set up just two years ago. Several mysterious objects have been reported this year, and I was briefly excited to find a newspaper report of a flying saucer that had actually crashed near Toulouse, complete with a picture of the craft and its pilot. It was only later that I noticed the date on the newspaper: April 1st.

So visiting aliens are not quite yesterday's news in France, although alien abductions seem to happen mainly in the United States for reasons we had better not think about. It is odd that aliens never seem to kidnap any really interesting specimens of humanity: Nobel prize winners, great artists, radio commentators, and the like. Those picked up by flying saucers seem not to be the most impressive examples of our species.

This is all routinely dismissed as crazy stuff, and yet how crazy is it? The universe is infinite, although it's hard to imagine that. One way to get your mind around the idea of infinity is to imagine walking across Kansas twice, but my way is to think about leaving the earth on the space shuttle, escape velocity 20,000 miles per hour, and just going on at that speed for a year, beyond the solar system, then another year, another ten, another hundred, another thousand, another million, another trillion years. After all that you would still be in the universe, with no end in sight. How do you expect it to end - with a white picket fence?

How likely is it that so much valuable real estate remains uninhabited, and that we on our speck of dust are the only intelligent things in it? Infinite means infinite, so on an unlimited number of stars with planets it must be true that there are an infinite variety of creatures, some of them smart enough to have learned the secret of Captain Kirk's warp drive so they can travel between the stars. Logically then it is probable, almost to the point of certainty, that some of these aliens have found us, homing in on old radio signals that travel endlessly through space. They have checked us out. Then, like a fisherman with a disappointing catch, they have tossed us back into the great sea of annoying and silly life forms that undoubtedly inhabit the universe, and continued on to look for something interesting.

We always refer to these hypothetical visitors as "intelligent aliens," but I think we have to reserve judgment about that. If news reports can be believed they have visited the South of France many times, and yet they didn't stay here. Was it the language, the rather rough local wines, the government, or perhaps the garlic that drove them away? Maybe yes, maybe no. Some of our neighbors are a little odd, and some are downright peculiar. It looks like a typical French village, but there may be aliens among us. Indeed we are aliens ourselves in the eyes of the French government, and oddities in the eyes of our neighbors, which means that we fit right in.

Chapter 22

Market Forces

We have to get up early on Monday, Wednesday, Friday and Saturday mornings. Those are the days when there is a food market in the village or in town. There is also a flea market on Sunday, and a book market on Thursday, which leaves Tuesday as the only day we can afford to lie in bed without the risk of missing something. My French class is scheduled early in the morning on Tuesday.

This daily reveille is almost worth it because the markets are worth it. As everybody knows you have to hit a market fast, soon after it opens because, unlike a supermarket, a local outdoor market runs out of things. If M. Bertrand brings six dozen fresh farm eggs to the market and sells six dozen, that's it. They came from the farm in his little white van. There is no giant refrigerated truck with ten thousand more eggs waiting in the background to replenish his stock, and in any case the hens deserve a break.

Within a radius of four or five miles we can buy directly from farmers, all kinds of artisans and artists, bakers, small wineries, cheese makers, and olive oil producers. There are perfectly good supermarkets too, but the open-air market is so much more fun. I hesitate to use the word "authentic," but the fact is that Shakespeare or even Socrates would have felt perfectly at home in any of these markets, while a supermarket would have seemed like a nightmare to them.

"Where does all this stuff come from?" they would have asked, and received *no* very satisfactory answer.

In a farmer's market you do know more or less where the stuff on sale comes from. You can locate the farm that grows the lettuces, and indeed they come with a liberal coating of soil from the field at no extra charge. You can see the vineyard that provides the wine, and even visit the chickens if M. Bertrand is in a good mood. The goat cheese seller is willing to introduce you to his very personable goats, and the man who sells mushrooms and truffles in season offers some bizarre objects that seem to come from another (very dirty) planet, but are absolutely delicious. Nothing is highly sanitized or packaged, and the market brings us very closer to our food source. The meat displays can turn a sensitive person into a vegetarian overnight.

Such markets may be an anachronism in an age of modern distribution, but you find them all over the world including in America where they seem to be having a kind of renaissance. But agribusiness and the international food industry are winning the market battle, of course. Most of us have to eat mass produced food most of the time, even though the health gurus constantly warn us against it. The local market products certainly *seem* healthier because they are more natural and closer to the source, but the evidence is not all that strong. Processed food is not entirely junk. I've been eating it all my life, and I don't know if I would survive without my daily dose of chemicals and pesticide traces. My body has adjusted to them, much as it has adjusted to air pollution and commercial television. We are more adaptable than we imagine. Is processed food killing me? Obviously it is, but *slowly*, that's the main thing. Meanwhile I have time to enjoy natural food from the market, whether it's good for me or not.

But small scale can coexist with big scale, and it's a luxury to have the choice. However we have to support the small and local side of things, because it is always at a competitive disadvantage. We have to get up early and buy things at the market if we want to keep the market. It's more than just a picturesque entertainment for tourists; it is one of the last living links with a vanishing world.

Chapter 23

Putting on Appearances

It is always difficult to avoid the bombardment of bizarre images from the big European fashion shows, especially those in Paris and Milan. When the designers wheel out their latest creations they want us all to know about them, although common sense and embarrassment would suggest that they should keep them hidden in a very dark closet. The newspapers are happy to oblige with free publicity, they love to report on these events. It's an excuse to publish special supplements full of color photographs and expensive advertisements, along with long and breathless reports from fashion correspondents about the internal battles and scandals of the fashion world.

All this is perfectly understandable from a commercial point of view, of course. The only question that remains is: are they all crazy, or is it just me? In my naïve way I assume that a fashion show should be about clothes, the way a car show is about cars or an agricultural show is about cows. But nothing resembling clothes seems to be on offer at these events. The scraps of material hung on the bodies of the unfortunate skeleton-like models are, if anything, costumes in the theatrical sense. A newspaper report from Milan features some costumes that would be perfect for, say, a fanciful amateur production of Shakespeare's *A Midsummer Night's Dream*, and others that would be appropriate for bondage movies, or even the circus. But there's nothing here remotely suitable for walking down a French village street on a chilly day in October. The local gendarmes are fairly lethargic, but they could scarcely ignore a provocation like that.

My questions are the same every year when the new fashions are announced: who wears this stuff, and where, and why? It would be logical to assume that the people who buy the latest styles would be those who take the trouble to go to fashion shows, the real *fashionistas.* But a close examination of the newspaper photographs with a magnifying glass reveals that the spectators lined up alongside what is all too appropriately called the catwalk are dressed in perfectly ordinary street clothes. If even the people who go to fashion shows aren't fashionable, then who is? The mystery remains, and even deepens as the creations of the *haute couture* industry become more peculiar every year.

Fashion is not a big issue in a French village, although there are dress rules. I am trying hard to live up to them. It's not that the men and women here are particularly smart, let alone fashionable, but they are *neat*, that's the word. Whenever they step out of the house they are fully and properly dressed, the women with their hair done and just a touch of makeup, the men with their faces shaved, hair trimmed, shoes polished. And it struck me that (apart from personal pride) this may be simply because we walk everywhere in the village, and inevitably meet people we know. If I want to drive I have to walk all over the village anyway to discover where I parked the car this time. Outside their homes almost nobody dresses sloppily, or runs to get the mail in a housecoat, or goes to the market in jogging clothes. We are all on show all the time. The whole village is a catwalk, exhibiting the very latest styles of the 1950s.

Fortunately this is my favorite period when it comes to masculine *Haute Couture*. My wardrobe consists mainly of practical but definitely unstylish clothes picked up in the local market, in shades of brown and gray so as to merge into the background. One of my less fortunate purchases was a black hooded jacket with what appear to be Korean gang symbols embroidered on it. People step over to the other side of the street when they see me wearing it because it is so ugly to look at. So I must assume that, if I have one fashionable garment in my wardrobe, this jacket is it.

Senior Moment

We were trying to buy tickets on French railways, hoping to fit in a quick trip to Paris between strikes, when the ticket agent fixed me with a suspicious gaze.

"Why do you not have a senior card?" she demanded.

Well, there are at least two answers to that. First, I never think of myself as a senior, and second we don't need the label "senior" when we have the perfectly good Anglo Saxon word "old" to describe this stage of life. After a short struggle to formulate either of these objections in French I agreed to accept a senior card. All that was necessary was some identification and a trip to the local photographer who used a special senior camera to take a picture that made me look about ninety-five.

This card entitles me to substantial discounts on the excellent French railway system, and it works. The train conductors check it carefully, comparing the photo with my face as if I might be some sly teenager trying to pass myself off as a septuagenarian. Usually I survive this test without difficulty.

The older citizens of France are treated very well. They get discounts on just about everything, although in fact it would make more sense to give discounts to *poor* people of any age. There is nothing about simply getting old that makes one worthy of a discount. But these privileges are fiercely guarded, including the privilege of retirement at the age of sixty, or even younger, with a full pension.

The government has been pushing a plan to keep people working until the age of sixty-two or sixty-three, and the opposition has been enormous. The campaign to save early retirement almost grew into a new French revolution. About three million people joined street demonstrations all over the country. These protests have been supported by many young people, and at first I found this puzzling. After all, their taxes are financing the huge burden of pensions, and when you are (say) twenty years old your own retirement seems infinitely remote, and even unbelievable. When I was twenty I never thought for a moment that I would become old enough to qualify for a senior card. But today's young protestors have more imagination than I did, or perhaps more optimism. They can anticipate slogging away for forty more years in some factory or office until they achieve the earthly paradise of early retirement, and the sudden addition of several more years of work seems intolerable and unfair.

It is a very emotional protest movement that ignores both economics and logic. It has been suggested that a genuinely fair retirement plan could be created, based on a sliding scale according to the type of work a person has done over his or her lifetime. Hazardous, exhausting and unpleasant jobs like repairing power lines or arresting criminals would qualify for very early retirement, followed by all the high-stress occupations that involve direct contact with the public, like doctors and social workers. The deeper a worker moves into the back office the later his or her retirement date would become: teachers would retire earlier than administrators, for example, and academics who write books on educational theory would never get to retire at all.

Such a plan is entirely in accord with the great French traditions of rationalism and equality which means that, in the real world of politics, it will get a resounding "NON!"

Chapter 25

This Old House

When in France we inhabit a small village house. The word "inhabit" is appropriate because these old stone houses have something of the feeling of cave dwellings, even if they are equipped with all modern conveniences on the inside. The village has been here for more than six hundred years. The first written mention of it by name occurs in 1152, by which date it was already well-established. The basic layout of the streets has not changed much from a map made in the sixteen hundreds, and the nearby town of Uzès has been home to Dukes of France for over a thousand years.

So naturally we were interested in the history of this place, who lived here, and what their lives were like. But it was hard to get any reliable information. Village houses were built for peasants and artisans, and don't appear in any written record. They have been built on, built over and renovated for hundreds of years, so there is no overall architectural style such as you might see in a church or a grand chateau. We have to rely on the clues we can get from the oldest parts of building itself, and on stories told by the neighbors and by our handyman Pascal.

These stories are notoriously unreliable. There is something about the history of houses that makes even normally honest people lose their moral bearings. A house, especially an old one, is a subject for romance, so the tales we hear have to be taken with a very large pinch of salt.

We can be sure of one thing: this house is seriously *old*. The popular Public Television show "This Old House" claims to be about renovating antique structures, but their Brooklyn Brownstones and Bostonian Arts and Crafts homes are brand new construction compared to our old house. Villagers built these places to last, using large chunks of granite, and because we are right in the middle of the village the house is supported on both sides by other equally solid and ancient structures

Based on the stone vaulting in the lowest part of the house we guess that it was built sometime in the 1700s. Animals were kept down there, and you can still see a stone drinking trough with an iron ring to tether the sheep or goats. Career opportunities were limited. The inhabitants may have worked in the vineyards or the olive groves, and supplemented their incomes with milk, cheese and wool from these animals. Also, from the nineteenth century, the village had a small industry of pipe making, which led to its present reputation as a center for ceramic artists.

So this old house has seen a lot of history: eight kings, the French Revolution, two emperors, two world wars, and five republics so far. When it was first built, Louis XIV the Sun King was living in splendor in his palace at Versailles, oblivious to the revolution that would sweep his royal descendants away, and in Paris intellectuals like Voltaire were fomenting the philosophical revolution called the Enlightenment. But, out in the country, life in villages like this must have been brutally hard, with hot summers, cold winters, backbreaking work, and not much in the way of entertainment apart from the occasional religious war.

At first the house seemed semi-sacred, just because of all that heavy history. I even hesitated to drill a hole in the wall to hang a picture, but I needn't have worried. The electric drill just bounced right off the granite, and I had to hang the picture somewhere else. These old houses survive for a reason. They don't yield to storms, floods, earthquakes, or temporary occupants with electric drills. They are here for the duration, whatever that duration may be.

Chapter 26

Formula Zero

D riving in France is never dull. On the big autoroutes we have the thrill of speed, and on the minor highways the threat of deep ditches and huge trees on both sides with no room to maneuver plus, of course, the other drivers. French drivers seem to welcome these challenges, and respond to them bravely. It's no accident that motor racing is a popular sport here. Every Frenchman, and far too many French women, regards him or herself as Formula One champion in training.

There is a certain universal fascination about motor racing. We all drive so we can imagine what it would be like to be on the track ourselves. Now racing drivers carry video cameras on their helmets we can see it too, and almost feel it. The most dramatic circuits are those that run through the streets of a town, like the one in Monaco not far from here. The circuit map tells us moment-to-moment what a driver has to do: along the straight in sixth gear, 175 mph, down to first gear for two hairpins at 30 and up to second for a right angle curve taken at 89 mph, and so on. It is an amazing demonstration of nerve and co-ordination.

But those of us who drive every day on ordinary French roads have developed our own special skills, especially in the narrow village streets, and sometimes I wonder how the celebrated Grand Prix drivers would face up to *this* challenge. For example if we imagine this village as an on-street racing track, like Monaco, and our little Peugot as a nine-hundred horsepower Formula One car, a typical circuit at maximum speed would go something like this.

When the starting flag drops nothing happens for five minutes while we extract car from very tight parking space beside the church. Grand Prix drivers never have to do this. Then off we go along the straight towards village center, almost into second gear and up to 10 mph before meeting a car coming the other way. The street is only eight feet wide, so we have to back up a hundred feet. We tackle the straight again, this time successfully, and take a sharp right at 1 mph (first gear) into the square where the war memorial is. But that road is completely blocked by the yellow post office van, and the driver has gone into the café for a drink. So it's into reverse again, turn around and take the even narrower road uphill to the town hall, where we make another a sharp right (still in first gear, about 2 mph) carefully avoiding the old ladies who sit outside their houses on this corner, with their feet sticking out dangerously into the road. Past the town hall a reckless driver might almost get into second gear, except for the cats. A whole tribe of them live on this stretch of road, and they own it. So we drive very carefully past the cats, which brings us to an extreme dead-slow sharp right turn, almost scraping the mirrors or both sides, then an equally sharp left fifty feet down the hill, and so on. You get the idea. On this Grand Prix track we never get out of bottom gear, unless it's to go into reverse, and we're still only half way round the circuit.

It's easy to see why so many French drivers dream of attaining glory on the race track. They have the skills, they have the courage, and they have the instant reactions that save them from catastrophe a dozen times a day. All they lack are the super-fast Formula One cars. Thank goodness they don't have super-fast Formula One cars.

Chapter 27

Life Among the Exiles

We spent a whole morning in a small restaurant listening to a talk about garbage. The sanitation manager of the town had kindly volunteered to speak to our group of foreigners as part of our education in everyday French.

It certainly was everyday French. This was vocabulary we could use. We might not be able to read Proust or Flaubert in the original but, after an hour of instruction on the science and sociology of garbage disposal in the town we were ready to go out and talk trash with any passing street cleaner.

The group of about twenty people who had gathered for this educational experience consisted of expatriates from half a dozen countries. There are a lot of foreigners living in southern Europe, most of them British, Scandinavian and Dutch refugees from the frozen north. But more and more Russians and East Europeans are moving in too, refugees from both the weather and the toxic politics at home.

They are interesting people and, being separated from their native languages and cultures, they socialize with one another. Food and wine are common interests, and English is the common language although you can have some surreal multilingual conversations. But most foreign residents are at least trying to learn French with varying degrees of success, and many of them are working in education or business. They form a kind of parallel universe, a *diaspora* of middle class people who think that living in the South of France is a pretty neat idea, which it is. They hang out in their favorite cafes, haunt the markets, and soak up the sun when there is any sun.

There is a hierarchy among the expatriates of course, and the long-time residents are at the top of it. They know the secrets we all need to know: the labyrinthine ways of the tax system, the real story about health care, the best place to buy wine, the truth about the winter weather, and so on. The rest of us are eager students of their hard-won knowledge.

We don't qualify as full members of the expat community. We are birds of passage, here today and on the wing tomorrow. Many others do the same, coming and going for a few weeks or months according to the rhythms of weather or work, or simply whim. People are always just leaving, for Holland or Turkey or Brazil, or just coming back.

There is something appealing and almost inspiring about the disconnected expatriate lifestyle. In a world obsessed with nationalism and borders this floating population seems to offer a model of what a peaceful global society could be like. We don't "belong" here, of course. But what the expats share is the feeling that it is rather nice *not* to "belong" anywhere, to be comfortable refugees on the face of the planet. When you belong to a place it possesses you, and imposes all kinds of obligations. There are far too many people who feel stuck in the place of their birth, or in some anonymous suburb where they happened to buy a home forty years ago. That's geographical slavery. It doesn't matter where you are or what language you try to speak, so long as you have good food, good company, and regular garbage collection. If you know a better recipe for universal peace and happiness I'd like to hear about it.

Chapter 28

The Day of Kindness

We woke up one Saturday to learn from the local paper that it was The Day of Kindness in France, *La Journée de la Gentillesse*. There wasn't much we could do about this right away, because my wife had already kindly bought me a croissant for breakfast, and I couldn't eat two. But there it was, the second annual National Day of Kindness. Anyone who has had dealings with French waiters or traffic policemen might agree that a little kindness would be a good idea and several campaigns of this sort, under various names, have been launched and forgotten over the past few years, mainly with the aim of making tourists feel more welcome.

The National Day of Kindness is not a government campaign but an initiative by a popular psychology magazine, which means that it comes with plenty of theories and statistics which are published in newspapers and magazines all over the country. For example, when asked: "In what situations do you find kindness most difficult?" the vast majority replied: "When I'm driving." That I can believe. Others found it hard to summon up kindly feelings at work, or with their families, or on public transport: nothing surprising there.

The local newspaper ran its own web survey to identify people in the region who are known for their kindness to others, and featured some of these paragons in its pages. Altogether it was a very positive and appealing campaign, and it would be nice to see more like it. Kindness is not fashionable these days, and perhaps it never was. It's seen as weak and feminine, and one of the surveys quoted in the paper backs up this prejudice. The question was: "What keeps you from being a kinder person" and more than half the respondents said it was because they were afraid of seeming feeble or vulnerable, or being laughed at. That's a sad commentary on human nature.

Too many things in our society conspire to make us wary of kindness: sports, war, videogames, and business. Boys learn early in life how not even to *look* like nice guys. High school students have already developed the swaggering style and the macho language that makes them seem intimidating, even when many of them are (as their parents know) just regular harmless kids inside. Then there's that awful phrase: "Nice guys finish last," with its explicit message that nasty guys are the winners. It's true that in a world full of wolves, sheep are likely to have a short and unhappy life. But that's not the fault of the sheep. It suggests to me that the wolves need a vegetarian diet plan and some therapy, starting perhaps with a Day of Kindness.

On the evening of the Day of Kindness, which was also as it happened a beautiful day, we went to hear a lecture at the local library. The speaker set out to explain in fairly elementary terms the differences between scientific facts on the one hand and unscientific beliefs on the other. The subtext was global warming, which is half science and half faith. But I was thinking about global kindness. I strongly believe that kindness is good, but I can't prove it, any more than I can prove that cats are smarter than human beings although all the evidence points in that direction. A Day of Kindness is an act of faith, an unscientific experiment with no identifiable result. Kindness cannot possibly do any harm, and may do a lot of good. The only way to find out is to try it.

Chapter 29

Time on Their Hands

The French government is engaged in a perpetual struggle to trim down the nation's generous social security entitlements. In particular nobody likes the proposal to raise retirement age from 60 (or even younger) to 62 or 63.

The government should consider the secondary benefits of early retirement. It allows huge numbers of fit and active men and women to be free from routine work and to do things that nobody else has the time or energy to do. Everywhere in France you find them engaged in volunteer teaching, running many kinds of social organizations, promoting music and the arts, growing organic foods, restoring houses, and being very active and involved grandparents. Far from being idle parasites, they make life better for everybody.

Having so many young-old people on the loose makes life more interesting. Consider this scenario, that unfolded right outside our front door. It started with the postman, who complained that our house number was too small. As he knew all the houses intimately we suspected there was a hidden message in this complaint, and there was. Almost every house in the village has a matching house number, hand painted in blue and pale yellow on a glazed pottery plaque about eight inches square. The street names have the same design; it's a kind of village signature. All these plaques are made by the same local potter in a tiny workshop by the church. Our house didn't have one, so obviously we had to get one.

When our house number was made by the potter I took two screws and attached it to the front door: big mistake. Our young retired neighbor Francois popped out of his house and told us that the plaque must be on stone wall to left, a much harder proposition that wooden door because it meant drilling into granite. I got my tools, and drilled into the granite. As I was about to finish the job Francois popped up again. My screws were too small, he announced, and he would bring bigger ones tomorrow. I put everything away and waited.

Next day Francois appeared with two enormous screws, far too big for the holes in the pottery plaque. Rather than get two smaller screws he spent half the morning delicately enlarging the existing holes with a file. Meanwhile Raymond, another young retiree, has appeared from across the street. I'm surprised it took him so long. We explained the situation. He was horrified. "You can't put it there, he said, it will be stolen. You have to put it there" (pointing to a place over the door, way above our heads). We all discussed the security issue. Francois won, on the grounds that his screws were longer than anybody else's.

Another day passed and Francois reappeared with huge drilling machine to make yet larger holes in the granite. A long discussion ensued, in the middle of the street, in which the main question is how pretty the plaque would look in this or that position. You might not expect these down to earth French village men to care much about "pretty" but it seems that they do. At last the plaque was attached, slightly chipped and not quite straight, in the prettiest place.

Everyone shook hands, and a tedious five minute chore had become a piece of street theater that occupied three elderly men harmlessly and happily for three days, which is surely much better than having them sit sadly and uselessly in front of a computer terminal in some dull office. And now the postman can find the house, although of course he could find it perfectly well before. Now he can *approve of* the house, which is much more important. And all this is thanks to the generous French tradition of early retirement. It's a great gift. Many people would like to give it to the President right now.

Chapter 30

The French Philosophy of Work

B efore we started living in the south of France for part of each year I had always imagined that time moved more slowly in those southern climes, and that people went about their lives in a more calm and relaxed way. Nothing could be further from the truth.

The village where we live is a nest of workaholics and insomniacs. My wife bravely gets up every day at some hideously early hour, and goes to the butcher, the newspaper shop and the baker. All these establishments are blazing with light and full of customers at an hour when my preferred activity is to cower in bed under the covers.

I 'm not allowed to stay in bed for long. We have repairs and restoration projects to do on the house, and workmen have a terrible habit of arriving at or before dawn. Our main man – I would call him a handyman if it wasn't an insult to his many talents – is Pascal. I think we engaged him because of his name. It's reassuring to have the services of someone named after the seventeenth century French mathematician and moralist Blaise Pascal, who gave us that remarkable book of philosophical reflections called *Pensées*, meaning "Thoughts." There must be some family connection, because our Pascal also likes to think. Confronted, for example, with some ancient and fragile electrical wiring, he stands like a statue for what seems like hours, calculating how to add a new appliance without exploding the whole system. Then he goes ahead and does it. Anything is possible for Pascal. Fix the collapsing three-hundred year old arched vault of the basement: no problem. Unravel the labyrinthine plumbing and restore it to order: no problem. Pascal thinks it out, like his famous ancestor

He's not the only contractor with philosophical leanings. French artisans take the opportunity of meeting foreigners as an occasion to debate their own opinions. The painter Gérard, after explaining the chemical qualities of paint and his theory of color at length, sat down for coffee and launched into a lecture about the impact of tourism on French culture.

But in between conversations they do get down to work. There are no timid concessions to health and safety: no goggles, no gloves, and no scaffold or harness for work on the slippery roof high above the street. There's no French term for "safety equipment" in my dictionary. It doesn't seem to be part of their philosophy. One of Pascal's more endearing qualities is that he never seems to have any tools at all. He arrives at the door empty-handed but then, like a large and amiable conjurer, produces hammers, saws, drills and brushes from his pockets, or from under his baggy gray sweater.

Because their lives are risky our workmen prefer to be paid in cash. They also want to save us the trouble of writing checks, and this is further evidence of their intellectual qualities. When the tax collector calls for his kilo of flesh the workmen will need to recall every transaction, every handful of used Euros stuffed into a back pocket throughout the year, in order to pay their proper tax share. It is an impressive feat of memory. Pascal and Gerald, and all the rest are a credit to the French education system. But, my goodness, they are tiring people to have around the house. It almost makes me want to do the work myself.

Chapter 31

House Book

Moving out of a house after a long stay is always a tedious affair. There's a vast amount of cleaning to be done, in the course of which many unfortunate discoveries will certainly be made: lost keys, lost papers, dead mice, and so on. There will be the painful triage when you decide what to take and what to leave behind. If you have been wearing the same few garments for months you either want to throw them or away or continue living comfortably in them forever. The latter decision will depend on your sex, of course. There are lots of small repairs to be attempted, and people we must absolutely say goodbye to, including really important ones like the butcher and the baker. But by far the most demanding task is preparing the house for those who will be coming to stay in it during the next few months, because this involves creating a "House Book."

A House Book is supposed to tell the next occupant everything he or she needs to know in order to have a safe and enjoyable stay, and not set fire to the place or allow it to be taken over by stray cats. Few House Books fulfill this task adequately. They tend to be either too brief and un-informative, with cryptic instructions like "Hot water may be obtained by activating the 20 amp breaker switch", without any indication of where in the house this object may be found, or they are maddeningly verbose and authoritarian, like an army drill manual written by Marcel Proust.

Creating one of these books is harder than it looks. Our old village house is nothing but a hollow cube of stone with a tiled roof. It has been around for some hundreds of years and could be destroyed only by a direct nuclear strike. In the old days goats were kept in the basement and rabbits in the attic, with the people living in between. In short the house is not a fragile object, like a piece of porcelain. There's nothing to worry about, or so you might assume.

But in this century builders and interior designers have done their transformative work, and now there are hundreds of things to worry about: heating systems, Internet connections a temperamental stove, idiosyncratic light fixtures and water filters, to name only a few. Oh for the simple life, as Thoreau described it! "Our houses are such unwieldy property that we are often imprisoned rather than housed in them," he wrote, with his usual irritating perspicacity.

I have tried to compose a House Book that will be comprehensive, informative, friendly in tone, and legally impregnable. It was an impossible task until I decided to write it from the visitor's point of view. They have questions, I have answers.

- What do we do about garbage? *Answer:* The rules of garbage disposal in a French village are beyond the understanding of any foreigner. Watch what the people next door do with their garbage, and do the same.
- The laundry machine looks funny – does it work? *Answer:* Yes, but there's nothing funny about it. Prepare for all your clothes to be the same color.
- Why are there five remote controls? *Answer:* Because there's French TV and British TV, and radio, coming from a satellite dish and an antenna and goodness knows where else, and I

haven't figured out how to make it all work with fewer than three remotes. The fourth and fifth remote are a surprise: try them and see.

- Where can I park? *Answer:* Keep driving until you get to the next village. They have parking.
- Where can I go for walks? *Answer:* Anywhere, except in hunting season, when it's best to stay home especially if you look even very slightly like a wild pig. The hunters don't discriminate.

The House Book, as it emerges on my keyboard, is a kind of model or blueprint of domestic life in France. It tells us how we should live, and by example tries to persuade others to live the same way. It's a good life, but only if you read the instructions.

Chapter 32

A Museum for All Ages

Museums and art galleries are wonderful places for self-education and self-improvement, but they are hard on the feet and on the brain. Few of us have enough knowledge to appreciate even a fraction of the exhibits in a typical museum. We spend the tour desperately scrabbling for faded scraps of memory, or false memory, about ancient Greek funeral rites or Mayan pottery. If it is a guided tour we stand numbly listening to long explanations that, however interesting, travel straight from one ear across to the other and out again.

It has been suggested by at least one ironic commentator that much suffering and boredom could be avoided if tourists were to be given an elementary test before they were allowed to enter these temples of high culture. It could be a very simple multiple choice. For example:

What city are you in right now?
(a) Florence
(b) Venice
(c) Pittsburgh
(d) The guide hasn't told us yet.

What famous work of art might you expect to see in the Louvre?

(a) Andy Warhol's soup cans

(b) The Mona Lisa

(c) The 1964 Ford Mustang

(d) Lady Gaga

But we feel morally obliged to make these pilgrimages into the past whenever they present themselves. For a tourist the word "museum" creates instant guilt, as much as the word "restaurant" creates instant hunger. So we do our duty, salute the past, and then head for the food.

Sometimes a special treat comes along. Way out in the French countryside we discovered a museum of toys and games. Instead of the hard slog of looking at things we only half understood, here was a museum where we could understand everything. The buildings, which admittedly were not quite as impressive as the Metropolitan Museum or the Uffizi Gallery, displayed some five thousand objects, most of them from the nineteenth and early twentieth centuries - not so far away in time as to be incomprehensible. If you are my age your grandmother was very familiar with the things on display in this museum.

A collection of toys and games is different from other collections. Just about everything in it conspires to make you happy. This one offered toys for all ages, from teddy bears and spinning tops to antique trucks, cars, motor cycles, fire engines, and even steam tractors. They also had a stuffed rabbit just like the one I had when I was a baby. Actually I still have him, but don't tell anybody.

There were all kinds of half-forgotten children's games without beeps or batteries, and we gazed nostalgically at hand-cranked home movie projectors, valve radios, glass plate cameras, and wind-up gramophones with big brass horns. It was no surprise to learn that this is the busiest museum in the region, with the single exception of a museum of candy a few miles away which is even more popular because it gives free samples.

We take ourselves far too seriously most of the time. We surely deserve a brief period of mindless pleasure like a warm bath or a happy dream. We'll get back to the Museum of Modern Art eventually, I promise.

Chapter 33

Dormouse in the House

Old houses in warm climates often serve as crash pads for birds, insects and other unauthorized creatures who make themselves very much at home without ever offering to share the mortgage payments. On the whole the human residents learn to live with their non-paying guests, but not always.

When we arrived in France this year it was clear that our tolerance was going to be tested. Some sort of wild all-night party was going on in the walls and roof of the house and we couldn't sleep at all. It sounded as if a herd of elephants or teenagers were trapped in there, but our neighbors reassured us that it was probably only a family of European Dormice or *Loirs*. This was not what we wanted to hear.

Everything I knew about dormice I had learned from reading *Alice in Wonderland*, where a dormouse played a major comic role in the Mad Hatter's Tea Party scene. He slept most of the time, but occasionally woke up to express some philosophical conundrum such as:

`You might just as well say,' "I breathe when I sleep" is the same thing as "I sleep when I breathe"!'

He also told an original story about two girls who lived in a treacle well, and lived on treacle while learning to draw. "They drew all manner of things, everything that begins with an M," said the dormouse, "Such as mouse-traps, and the moon, and memory, and muchness - you know you say things are 'much of a muchness' - did you ever see such a thing as a drawing of a muchness?" Then he fell asleep again.

You can see that this was an entertaining dormouse, so much so that he had to be suppressed by putting him in a teapot.

Now I could live with, and even learn to like such whimsical, ironical dormice but ours told no jokes and proposed no riddles. They just scratched and squeaked. Reasoned arguments and threats of legal action didn't disturb them, even in French.

The stories we read when we're very young, and no doubts the movies we watch too, color our thoughts about the animal kingdom for a lifetime. The gentle cast of otters, moles, mice, squirrels, bears and ducks that populate the tales of childhood make it hard to think of the creatures in any other way. But we tried. We hardened our hearts against the dormice, reminding ourselves that the Romans used to eat them, marinated in honey, and that in any case they are just rats with cute faces and bushy tails.

My idea was to live trap the dormice and carry them off to the nearby woods where they wouldn't disturb anybody. But our neighbors, who shared the wall and its menagerie, wanted nothing to do with live traps. An exterminator was called, and the dormice turned out to be rats – very large rats.

Rats don't get such a good press. They are associated with sewers and diseases, with the Pied Piper of Hamelin, with the phrase "You dirty rat." There are not many fine or heroic rats in fiction, but why not? I could cite Remy, the talented rat in the animated film *Ratatouille*, and the literary rat in *Firmin* who lived in a bookstore and educated himself by eating the books. Also I had a pet white rat I was very fond of when I was a kid. Soon I began to feel as sorry for the rats as I had for the dormice.

But there was no stopping the exterminator and the rats have fallen silent. We can sleep peacefully all night, and I still feel terrible about it.

Chapter 34

Revolution Now

*B*astille Day is hard to miss if you happen to be in France. There are parades and patriotic speeches in every town and village, and often fireworks and festive dinners too. This year's celebration marked the two hundred and twenty-fourth anniversary of the French Revolution, and it had a special poignancy because of the ongoing turmoil in Egypt. Revolutions have a way of going wrong, or going nowhere, but this doesn't seem in any way to diminish their popularity. The Arab Spring has produced a whole series of popular uprisings after 2010, with no clear result except mounting chaos and religious wars.

The tempting thing about a revolution, as compared say to an election or a Congressional enquiry or a grass roots campaign, is that it promises big changes right now. Also, very importantly, it promises that *your* kind of people will finally be in charge and *their* kind of people will be out in the cold, or dead – us versus them, winner takes all. The expectation is that *your* people will certainly give you whatever you want, whatever it is. But so often, as in George Orwell's parable *Animal Farm*, once *your* people are in power they turn out to be exactly like *their* people, or worse. If you have absolutely no knowledge of history this always comes as an unpleasant surprise.

Fine slogans like "No taxation without representation" tend to vanish in a puff of smoke right after the revolution. Every government adores taxation. Other resounding slogans like "Freedom now" or "Liberty, Equality, Fraternity" are rarely given the kind of rigorous sociological examination that would perhaps make the revolutionaries think twice. Too often they don't think at all, being absolutely convinced that their religion, tribe, economic system, or political party is the only right and virtuous one, and that any contrary argument or evidence is a waste of time, and probably wicked into the bargain.

The closest I ever got to a revolution was in 1968, when I was able to observe the so-called youth revolution as it unfolded in London, Paris, and Berkeley, California. It was all very dramatic, but even at the time it seemed more like performance art than politics. In the end it produced some positive change by challenging a lot of outdated prejudices. But on the negative side you could argue, and plenty of clever people have argued, that the events of those years deepened the huge political and cultural divide that is now one of our main problems: us versus them.

Revolutions are always ambiguous. The French revolution produced first chaos and bloodshed, then the dictatorship of Napoleon, then a return of the monarchy in 1815, and finally a democratic republic thirty-three years later. Revolutionaries rarely want to wait that long. A revolution, like a music festival, is about enthusiasm – what's happening now rather than what may happen later. It's about the experience of being there, and sharing the excitement.

You might say: so much for revolutions, they're nothing but trouble. But here's the catch – and don't blame me, it was Thomas

Jefferson who said it: "What country can preserve its liberties if their rulers are not warned from time to time that their people preserve the spirit of resistance?" Without the occasional messy rebellion, Jefferson believed, nothing would ever change.

Chapter 35

Vive le Roi

July 14th is Bastille Day, a holiday that commemorates the ambiguous legacy of the revolution of 1789. This was the date when the people of Paris, or a few hundred of them, stormed the prison called *La Bastille*, and released a rather disappointing total of seven political prisoners. This rebellion led directly to the Declaration of the Rights of Man. Authoritarian regimes everywhere have learned from these unfortunate events to keep their political prisoners in remote and inaccessible places. The old Bastille prison is long gone, but this is still a very significant site for Parisians who remember any history prior to yesterday's lunch.

Bastille Day seems superficially similar to the Fourth of July: there are flags, there are fireworks, there are speeches – and everybody goes to the beach. But it's really a very different kind of celebration. The Fourth is about national independence and patriotism, but the fourteenth was really a revolution of the poor against the rich, especially against the king and the aristocracy.

After Bastille Day in 1789 there was a period of anarchy called The Terror, symbolized by the guillotine. King Louis XVI was tried and executed, and France fell into chaos. I was talking to my French teacher about this, or rather she was talking to me while I tried to say as little as possible.

We were discussing the old, unresolved question about how much power any one ruler should have. You may remember from college an English philosopher called Thomas Hobbes who in 1651 published a book called *Leviathan*, now a classic, in which he argued that our only security lies in giving absolute power to one individual – a king, an emperor, a dictator – who will protect us from external threats and, just as important, from each other. Remove the absolute ruler and anarchy is the result. This is what happens on a smaller scale when a strict teacher steps out of the classroom for a moment and the kids explode into total disorder. In Thomas Hobbes's view we were all unruly children who could not be trusted for a moment without strict supervision.

That is a standard conservative argument, but it's hard to avoid comparing the French Revolution with the Arab Spring that turned so quickly into winter. Repressive dictators fell all over the region, and look what happened next: the kids went wild. Plato made this argument a long time ago, and even Winston Churchill was skeptical about the benefits of popular rule. "The best argument against democracy," he grumbled, "Is a five-minute conversation with the average voter." In a newspaper interview, M. Roger de Prévoisin the leader of the Royalist Party of France, claimed that a king – a real king - would bring the whole disorderly country together and restore its former glory.

We're not really supposed to even think about the subversive appeal of an absolute ruler, especially not if we are lucky enough to live in a democracy. But it's one of those political conundrums that has not been solved in four hundred years, so at least it's worth a moment of reflection, especially on Bastille Day. Order and freedom pull in opposite directions: there's no getting around it, unless we find a way to change human nature.

I had to write an essay on the return of the monarchy for my French class. This was what I wrote (in French) and my teacher didn't like it. Some old-fashioned liberal republicans are just never satisfied.

Chapter 36

Feel My Pain

*E*verybody loves a mountain, especially if they can drive up to the summit instead of climbing. The most popular and highest mountain in the south of France is called Mount Aigoual, standing a little over five thousand feet, which has two excellent roads leading to the top. Our little Fiat just made it, and we were rewarded with a spectacular panorama. What took away some of the pleasure was the pain and suffering of the many cyclists who, for mysterious reasons of their own, had decided to *ride* all the way up the mountain, a distance of twenty-two miles, not a single one of them flat. There were dozens of cyclists, perhaps hundreds, all bathed in sweat with agonized faces and leg muscles that stood out like steel cables at breaking point. Nobody as far as I know was forcing them to do this, it was their own choice.

I can see that coasting *down* the mountain would be fun, When I was a kid my friends and I used to ride to a nearby hill and puff our way up to the top, just so we could come zooming down again. But our hill was only about a quarter of a mile long, probably no more than fifty feet high at the summit. That was all the pain and suffering we needed at that or any other age.

Human nature is unfathomable, although Sigmund Freud among many others tried to fathom it. Psychologists have long recognized the existence of masochism, the ability to get pleasure from pain. It seems to explain a lot about human nature, although we might be happier if it explained less. The world is full of examples. In addition to the cyclists we saw people actually *walking* the twenty-two miles up that mountain, carrying heavy backpacks. The trek takes eight hours. The diagnosis seems obvious.

Painful activities are extraordinarily popular – marathon running, all kinds of athletics, eating healthy diets, camping, and so on. I read about a forty-six mile off-road triathlon in Sweden that must be a kind of benchmark for miserable experiences. "It's about taking as much pain as possible," said one of the organizers. Indeed enthusiasts like to say "Feel the pain" with a kind of pride. But plenty of people with arthritis feel the pain – there's no virtue in it.

Pain is not a pleasure only for young people. Before climbing the mountain in our Fiat we had visited a famous spa nearby. This offered cures for just about everything, including old age, with a combination of sulfur baths and massage, with the additional option of being covered in honey as a special treat. The mixed stink of sulfur and honey in the place was quite literally nauseating, so we only stayed long enough to see a row of already-processed victims, people at the other end of life but still keen to suffer, sitting hollow-eyed on plastic chairs, wrapped in white robes, and obviously glad that it was all over.

This may be the answer of course. We enjoy suffering when it stops, when we get to the top of the mountain or climb out of the sulfur bath. It's the anticipation of relief that gives us courage, and the anticipated sense of superiority. Not me, I don't like pain. I go to considerable lengths to avoid it. But am I missing out on the pleasure of pain? Should I be torturing myself, just for the fun of it? It's the kind of question that gives me a headache, but an aspirin should take care of that.

Chapter 37

Tourism by the Numbers

Summer brings the tourists flocking into France like an invading army. The roads are full of little Dutch caravans going at forty miles an hour, and big Mercedes with Belgian plates going at a hundred and ten.

It is often said that tourism is the continuation of war by other means. The history of Europe had been an endless succession of wars and invasions. The French struggled mightily to keep out the British in 1453, and succeeded. They struggled to keep out the Germans in 1914 and 1939, and failed. Now, there are places in France where practically the only languages you hear spoken are English and German.

Tourism has many advantages over outright war. It is far less violent, and slightly less damaging to the environment. It is also very good for the collapsing French economy. Instead of fighting to keep us foreigners out, they welcome us in and sell us hotel rooms, meals, wines, expensive museum tickets and overpriced souvenirs. Even the old enemies have become valued customers.

A lot of the visitors are high school students from all over the world enjoying an educational tour. "Enjoying" and "educational" may both be the wrong words to use here. In high season in Avignon, our local tourist town, I can truthfully say that I have never seen so many bored, unhappy and rebellious young people gathered together in one place since the last time I taught a college class. The only things that seemed to attract their attention were the pizza and ice cream stands, video game arcades, and Internet cafes, which are strategically placed along the main tourist routes. The Internet cafes are almost redundant of course. Every teenager comes fully wired to the Internet, and seldom disconnects. These so-called educational tours may be fun for the teachers, although their haggard faces make me doubt it. I'm certain that they are counter-productive for the students, who probably learn only to detest beauty and culture for the rest of their lives.

I have mixed feelings about mass tourism, because I'm a part of it. Everybody should be able to see unique and wonderful places like Paris and Florence. But, with six billion people in the world, we can't do it without destroying the places we want to see. Venice is the worst. Soon they will need pushers, like those on the Tokyo subway, just to shove people into Venice.

In its earlier days tourism was about seeing new places and learning from them. Now the social media have changed the equation and the world has become no more than a background. The individual has moved center stage. "Here's me, and that's the Mona Lisa behind me." The narcissistic craze for selfies and video clips seems to encourage crazy or boorish behavior just so that the moment can be recorded and posted online. The portability of cameras makes it all too easy. You wouldn't set up a big, complicated two thousand dollar Nikon camera just to snap yourself doing something idiotic in the streets of a foreign city, but in the drunken moment with cell phone in hand it probably seems like a good idea. Then you can share it with all your friends on the web, and live with the embarrassment forever. It will probably still be there for your own children to find.

The Roman poet Horace divided all travelers into two groups: those who travel for a change of climate, and those who travel to change their minds. But, as G.K.Chesteron wrote: "They say that travel broadens the mind, but first you must have the mind."

Chapter 38

Where Am I?

When I need to find my way around in this complicated world my navigation system, which has always served me well, consists of a collection of tattered maps and street guides, some of them dating back to the 1960s, and a small pocket compass that points randomly in all directions.

The opportunity to move into a new age of technology came this summer with a car rental that included, as part of the contract, a free portable global positioning system. This turned out to be a little gadget, half the size of a folded road map, with an even smaller set of instructions printed in smudged ink on a scrap of paper, and apparently translated from the Chinese by somebody whose first language was Swedish.

However this was a brand new, state of the art, twenty first century GPS, and I couldn't wait to try it. But I didn't throw away my maps quite yet, which was just as well. A paper map shows you the way and takes you right there. The makers of GPS systems have decided that this is much too easy. First you need to persuade the machine to recognize where you want to go, even though you yourself know this already. Your GPS also knows the one and only right way to get there, and will not change its tiny electronic mind, so forget about any creative diversions. If you prefer to use an unconventional route to avoid traffic, for example, or to view some attractive scenery, you are out of luck.

When I plugged in the GPS it thought it was in Wisconsin and had to be convinced that it was actually in France. Then, as a test, I asked to be guided to the nearest town a few miles away, on a road I knew well. It demanded a street name and number, which I didn't have, then offered half a dozen towns with similar names that I might perhaps prefer to visit. Finally, grudgingly, it allowed me to move off, speaking in a flat, authoritarian voice that sounded like a Midwestern school teacher. She had not studied the language of the country she was in, and pronounced the names phonetically which made them entertaining but incomprehensible.

She got me on to the right road, after a great deal of what she called "re-calibrating," but it was good that I already knew the way because my electronic guide had little sympathy for human foibles, or even for geographical reality. When I took a small detour into a village she ordered: "Stop, turn round." This was in a village street eight feet wide where I had no more prospect of turning than of flying, and that was a one-way street in any case.

The GPS lit up with enthusiasm whenever we approached a gas station, in spite of the appalling prices, but she did not warn me of really important things like speed limits, lurking gendarmes, mad teenagers, or sheep on the road. She was far from infallible. On the return journey, which she did not seem to enjoy, she ordered me to turn right into the front window of a pharmacy instead of left into the main street.

The car and its navigation system went back to the rental agency, and I went back to my collection of moth-eaten maps. Maps worked for Columbus, more or less, and for all the great explorers down to recent times. I may soon be the last person in the world to use a paper map, but I may also be the last to actually know where I am.

Chapter 31

The Knowledge Man

We always forget to celebrate this important moment in intellectual history. Denis Diderot was born on October 5, 1713 in France. This may not seem like the most dramatic piece of news to hear three hundred years after the event, but every time Mr. Google, Wikipedia, or any of the online search engines answers one of our questions we are benefitting from the vision and determination of Monsieur Diderot.

His idea, which was as simple as it was brilliant, was to gather together all the knowledge in the world in a systematic way so that anybody could find information about anything. In other words, Diderot invented the encyclopedia.

It was a project on a heroic scale, completed in 1772 and filling twenty-seven large volumes containing seventy-five thousand entries. It was not at all popular among the rich and powerful of the time. The idea of spreading knowledge is never welcomed by people whose position depends on the ignorance of those less fortunate. Knowledge really is power. That's why universal education evokes such mixed feelings. On the one hand it is an engine of economic progress. On the other, once people start thinking for themselves who knows what might happen?

Diderot was said to have written ten thousand of the Encyclopedia articles himself. Some of them were so radical that the entire book was banned for a while. But now it is treated as an intellectual monument, and the French state honored the author in his centennial year.

When I was growing, up encyclopedia salesmen came from door to door. "The encyclopedia man" became a kind of joke, spoofed by Monty Python among others. My parents had two different sets in multiple volumes, one for adults and one for children – that is to say, for me, my very own encyclopedia. An encyclopedia in the house was supposed to guarantee that your child would grow up both intelligent and knowledgeable, and obviously it worked in my case. You can still find printed encyclopedias gathering dust in public libraries, but rarely on family bookshelves. Now we have the glorious, infallible Internet at our fingertips. It remains to be seen whether the Internet in the house will guarantee that your child will grow up both intelligent and knowledgeable.

The great thing about an encyclopedia in book form, and especially a big one like Britannica or Americana, is that you can read it, explore it, and get lost in it. One thing leads to another, and another, and another. You may start by looking up (say) Diderot and end up reading about speculative fiction. I know, because it happened to me. Internet search engines simply seek out a target and hit it: here's your question, here's your answer, end of story. This is very practical and useful, but there's no adventure in it, and precious little chance of making any strange or unexpected discoveries.

Intellectual giants of the past like Goethe, Nietzsche, Hegel, and Freud all admired Diderot, not just for his massive encyclopedia but for his subversive satirical writing. He was a man with a mission to promote knowledge in all its forms without prejudice and without censorship. It is ironic to reflect that if he were to pursue the same passion now, three centuries later, he would probably be in as much trouble with the authorities as he was then.

Chapter 40

A Real Bargain

The French economy is in a poor state. Everyone is looking for bargains, and there are plenty to be had if you don't insist on shopping in regular stores. As soon as summer arrives every village or group of villages has a *vide grenier* (literally the emptying of the attic). In the suburbs of Connecticut and Long Island we see plenty of two or three family yard sales. Try to visualize a two hundred family yard sale. People bring their junk and treasures from miles around and spread them all over the local market place or village park. It is like the biggest, craziest and tackiest department store you ever imagine, and absolutely addictive. Electronics, toys, books, DVDs, tools, furniture, and clothes are all on sale for next to nothing. We were restrained last weekend and came away with no more than two paperbacks, but we could and we have practically furnished a whole house from sales like these.

Last week I needed something to wear. I had packed for the trip in my usual haphazard fashion, leaving out things that my wife assured me were essential for comfort and respectability in a climate that can switch from hot to cold when you least expect it. The village yard sale did not provide exactly the right thing, and we were advised to try a used clothing establishment that everyone agreed was the very best place to buy clothes, as long as you weren't too picky and not in too much of a hurry. When we found it this fashion emporium proved to be a large dilapidated shed on the edge of a field. The door was chained shut from the inside, but the bell brought an elderly woman who unchained it while hanging on to a large dog with one hand to keep him from getting out. He wasn't a fierce dog, in fact he was excessively friendly, but for every customer who went in or out of the store the owner had to go through the chaining and unchaining ritual. As she was also running the checkout this slowed things down considerably.

The dark interior of the store was an exploding mass of clothing of every possible kind, from witch's hats to ball gowns, in apparently no order whatsoever. After a longish search we found what I needed – two jackets, both a perfect fit - for less than the cost of a couple of bottles of wine. The door was unchained, we had said goodbye to the dog and the owner, and slipped out into the sunshine, a couple of very satisfied customers. You can keep the big fashion stores of Paris, that's what I call proper French shopping experience.

Chapter 41

Modestine Forbids

The international tourist industry offers many pre-packaged cultural experiences. Some of these experiences are more strenuous than others, and therefore easier to resist. For example, if you drive through a range of gentle mountains in southern France called the Cévennes, you will be astonished at the number of places that offer donkey rides. This is not just a piece of fun. It is all the fault of the Scottish writer Robert Louis Stevenson, who is best remembered for those splendid adventure stories *Treasure Island* and *Kidnapped*, and for the dark, Freudian fantasy of *Dr. Jekyll and Mr. Hyde*. He was also a fine travel writer, and in 1878 he took an eleven-day hike through these very hills with an obstinate donkey called Modestine. The result was a charming little book called *Travels with a Donkey in the Cevennes*, which I discovered and loved when I was about twelve years old.

Stevenson's book has created a whole donkey trek industry. Many tourists in these mountains actually do hire donkeys in order to relive his experience properly. Little groups can be seen setting off into the woods, the donkeys loaded down with camping equipment and food for the journey. The opinions of the donkeys about this are not recorded. But much as I like donkeys I didn't want to ride one for eleven days, and nor did my wife. So we followed Stevenson's route by car, reliving his experience as it were on fast forward in a single day.

This, of course, was nothing but self-delusion. Stevenson and Modestine walked a total distance of about a hundred and twenty miles. They were often lost, often misdirected by peasants, and they slept in horrible inns without cable TV or hot water. Sometimes they were forced to camp in the open, in the rain. Stevenson had plenty of time to think. Indeed, he traveled alone quite deliberately, so that he *could* think.

His was a type of journey almost forgotten: a philosophical journey. His mental companions were writers like Laurence Sterne, William Hazlitt and Henry David Thoreau. Not many tourists in the Cévennes today carry this kind of intellectual baggage. Stevenson was fascinated by the geography of the region, by the aesthetic quality of the landscape, and also by the religious character of the people who lived there. This was and is the heartland of French Protestantism, so its history interested the Scottish author very much. The light relief in the book is provided by the difficult personality of the donkey Modestine, their joint misadventures, and the people they met along the way.

Stevenson wrote: "I travel not to arrive at any particular place, but for the simple pleasure of travelling." This meditative experience is precisely what we modern tourists miss. When you are going at hundred kilometers an hour on mountain roads, and surrounded by French drivers, any form of meditation or even thought would be suicidal. So although we followed Stevenson's route, and saw the same villages and landscapes that he saw more than a century ago, I can't pretend that we had any deep philosophical experiences as a result. But I'm glad we did it. We saved ten whole days on the journey, the scenery was incomparable, I re-read to Stevenson's book with new understanding and respect, and best of all no donkeys were inconvenienced in the course of researching this essay.

Chapter 42

The Sunshine Lifestyle

*E*very summer the countries around the Mediterranean welcome (if that is the right word) a great migration of about three hundred million tourists from the dismal north. They flap and flutter across the beaches and through the streets of the picturesque villages wearing those strange bright clothes that tourists are expected to wear so they don't get mistaken for normal people.

The citizens of Northern Europe normally suffer a horrible winter followed by a miserable spring, so the impulse to get away is overwhelming, even if only for a week or two, to cast off dull clothes and inhibitions, eat in outdoor cafés, breathe outdoor air, and just play. But of course a brief taste of paradise is never enough. A little sunshine is a dangerous thing, because it offers a glimpse of a different life.

The natural desire to live in an outdoor climate, which I totally share, has created a whole aspirational lifestyle fantasy. Why not live like this all the time? In fact seven out of ten British people want to leave the country permanently and head south. There are half a million of them already in Spain alone. Sunny and happy TV shows constantly reinforce the desirability of life in southern Europe, or Australia, or Dubai, or just about any spot on the weather map where it stops raining occasionally.

Northern Europeans who move to the south to live don't always get what they bargained for. They have exchange rate worries, tax puzzles, real estate scams, health care surprises, and swimming pool problems. Pools are a major preoccupation of the expatriate community. In a warm climate they can grow strange life forms unknown to biology if you are not liberal with the chemicals. A pool in the sunny south also acts as a magnet for all your friends and relatives, and their children and grandchildren, so for the resident the experience is less like lifestyles of the rich and famous and more like running a free hotel. Routine things like shopping and driving can be a challenge in a foreign country, and after a while the expatriates will discover the awful truth that there is indeed a winter in the south, and that it can be quite nasty. There is also the uncomfortable fact that moving to Europe often means having to learn a new language. Does any grownup person really want to spend several hours a week in a hot classroom being humiliated by an impatient young language teacher?

So if the sunshine lifestyle is a secular version of paradise, it conceals a whole nest of serpents. But for those who have achieved it the real payoff is not swimming in a green pool or wearing shorts for months at a time. The real payoff is in *not* being a tourist. However long their vacations, the tourists all must return in September, and here the phrase "The Return" has a very particular meaning. It always means a return to the north, not the east, west or south. "The North" is a package that contains rain and responsibility, school and work, gray skies, and upper respiratory infections. Who wants to go there?

Like the happy denizens of Florida or southern California, those who actually live in the sunshine zone of Europe have the satisfaction of watching the tourists leave. I don't know what they call this in Florida, but in France they call it *schadenfreude*.

Chapter 43

Tour de Force

One year the Tour de France came right through our village, generating huge excitement. This extraordinary bicycle race, which began back in 1903, covers a punishing course of about two thousand miles in three weeks all over France. Spectators need a certain amount of patience, and endurance too if the sun is hot. The riders are preceded by a long line of police, advertising and press vehicles, known as the "Publicity Convoy," and are followed by an equally impressive train of cars and trucks carrying spare parts for the bicycles and (one hopes) for the riders too. It all takes a long time and the riders themselves, once they appear, come and go in a flash. Like riots and natural disasters, the Tour de France is best enjoyed on television.

My father went in for bicycle racing when he was young, although I never did. It was as much as I could do to pedal the four miles to school and back every day, uphill in both directions. His old racing bike, which he kept for decades, was a miracle of simplicity – two wheels, an iron frame, and one brake. There were no gears, and no freewheel so the rider couldn't stop pedaling even for a second. Old family photos suggest that my father's generation went racing in their everyday clothes, minus jackets, with no more safety equipment than a cloth cap.

Things have changed. Modern racing cyclists resemble creatures from another planet. They look almost like insects, as my wife remarked, with their restless legs, bright dangerous colors, surreal helmets, and tiny black goggles. Their super high-tech machines are no more like regular bicycles than Formula One race cars are like your family sedan. Competitive cycling seems to be an all-male activity, perhaps a kind of bonding ritual and, as in most male sports, the cute outfits and the expensive equipment are a big part of the attraction.

Cycle racing is a national sport in France, but you seldom see a solitary rider any more than you see a solitary starling. They are usually found hurtling along in tight packs, like hunting dogs, and unlike anything else on French roads they seem to possess a semi-sacred status, rather like cows in India. Cyclists must not be harassed, hooted at or told to move over, let alone run over by impatient motorists. The Tour de France causes enormous disruptions to traffic, as miles of roads are closed for each daily stage, but nobody complains.

On race day a motley crowd gathered at convenient spots along the route around the village. Because this was France everyone was well supplied with food and bottles of wine, and impatient to see the riders as they flew past in a blur of colors on their way to the grand finale in Paris. My legs and many other parts of my anatomy ached in sympathy. But I told myself: they don't have to do it. Riding in the Tour de France is not fate, but choice. The symbolic yellow jersey is the ultimate prize for a cyclist, although it takes an almost superhuman feat of strength and endurance to win it. I'm glad we were there to cheer them on. Madness on this scale deserves recognition, and respect.

Chapter 44

The Slow Train

As we were leaving for France, a thoughtful friend gave us an old Baedeker guide book. This famous German series has been published since 1827, but this was a relatively recent edition from 1907. Studying its closely printed pages and exquisite maps, we were transported back into the entirely different Europe that existed before the two World Wars.

An historic guide book like this is the next best thing to a time machine. There's no mention of air travel, of course, and scarcely any reference to automobiles or road trips, except to warn the reader how dangerous they are. Travel in those days meant mostly train travel, and it had many advantages. It was cheap and energy efficient. You didn't need to get a driving license, or make an investment of thousands of dollars in a car and insurance. The social class system was rigorously maintained, with first, second and third class carriages, which may seem old-fashioned until you remember the equally sharp class divisions of modern air travel. There were also ladies' carriages, sleeping cars, and smoking cars. Best of all, your luggage was taken care of from start to finish. There was no need to carry it, or even touch it.

If you are a fan of the Sherlock Holmes series on public TV – the old one with Jeremy Brett not the new flashy one – you will have noticed that Holmes is forever studying timetables and rushing to catch trains. He even pursued the wicked Professor Moriarty by train, puffing through Switzerland in a parody of a car chase. This was possible because trains in those days were not just commuter links between cities and suburbs. They went everywhere, even to small villages, where you can still find the ghostly, long-abandoned stations. The Baedeker guide offers almost a hundred tours and excursions, and each tour starts with the words: "From the station…"

You can follow these old routes in a shadowy way if you don't mind some hard walking. The little local trains have long gone, and the iron tracks have been ripped up. But the rail beds remain, wandering through the landscape, over bridges and through long dark tunnels, providing a spectacular way for the determined hiker to see the countryside far away from the main roads. .

We used to take our daily walk on the old railway when we lived near Montpellier, and now I see from the Baedeker that it was part of a line that ran thirty-seven miles from Montpellier to Lodève, both small towns in those days. It was a three hour journey with five stops. Now you can do it by car in an hour, and use the other two hours looking for a place to park.

The French destroyed their local rail network long ago, as did the British. The era of the private car had arrived and nothing could stop it. A car is a capsule, just like home. There's no need to keep a timetable, or to interact with strangers. Family feuds can be kept in the family. In short, when it comes to privacy, there's no contest.

So the slow train has gone the way of the transatlantic liner and the horse and carriage, leaving only these old guide books to remind us of an age when not everyone – Sherlock Holmes excepted – was in such a perpetual, anxious hurry.

Chapter 45

A Lot of Bulls

*I*f you travel in southwestern France or Spain during the summer months you will probably pass through a town that is celebrating its annual *Fête Votive* or *Encierro*. The best advice I can give is to continue passing by and drive right on to the next town.

For a long time I was under the illusion that a *Fête Votive* was a religious festival, perhaps because the name suggested votive candles. But that's not it at all: when you see *Fête Votive* think "veal," because this is a festival dedicated cattle, and more particularly to running bulls through the streets.

The historical explanation of this curious activity is that, before the days of cattle trucks when bulls had to be transported from place to place, they were herded by men on horses, like cowboys, or bully boys in this case. When the herd came to a town or village it was important to prevent the bulls from drifting off into side streets, upsetting café tables and causing trouble in china shops. So the herd was whipped up to a gallop and closely confined by the horsemen to get them all through town as fast as possible. As time went by this bull running became a kind of a spectacle and a game. Young men would show their courage by running with or ahead of the bulls. This is because, not to put too fine a point on it, young men are very stupid. Young women do not do this.

This curious custom has persisted long after it had any practical purpose, and is now an institution. Pamplona in Spain is probably the most famous example, but almost every town in the southwest seems to have a bull-oriented festival. Testosterone-crazed followers like Hemingway have found these events exciting, and even a kind of art. But because the bulls are huge black monsters with long sharp horns, and in a bad temper, they can do a lot of damage. Every year the local newspapers publish lists of young men injured or even killed all over the region during these bizarre events, and there is beginning to be a discussion about whether running dangerous bulls through populated areas is a good idea. No conclusions have been reached so far on this difficult question, although in France sixty per-cent of the population are against it. The other forty per-cent defend it as a "tradition," and that's what counts. Not coincidentally it also brings in the tourists.

Some of the bulls used in these affairs are intended for the arena, and indeed the *Fête Votive* is culturally part of the even more unpleasant bull fighting culture. The only difference is that you don't have to be a toreador to get trampled and killed in the *Fête Votive*. This is equal opportunity madness.

The *Fête Votive* is more than just a load of bulls. It is a saturnalia. There is music and dancing and an enormous amount of drinking. Normally we leave our car on the street, but kind neighbors offered to shelter it in their courtyard during the local festival, warning that the car might not survive otherwise. A lot of people simply leave town for a few days, as they probably did in the old west when the cowboys came through.

In short, the festival of the bulls is colorful, lively, dangerous, and cruel to animals and people. Quaint old customs like this are truly the stuff of history, and history is where they belong.

Chapter 46

Ancient History

The romance of the past is much easier to enjoy because we are anchored firmly in the present. We can imagine the past, by way of books and movies, and even catch a glimpse of the real thing by viewing the ruins left behind by vanished civilizations. But we wouldn't want to live there.

History weighs more heavily in Old Europe, because there is so much of it and its traces are so monumental that no visitor can ignore them. Great castles and fortresses dot the landscape from Spain to Scandinavia. We've been touring in a part of France not far from the Spanish border, which is particularly rich in such massive ruins.

This region has an absolutely dreadful history. Leaving aside the prehistoric period, which must have been very nasty indeed, it was occupied successively by the Greeks and the Romans, the Vandals and Visigoths from Germany and the Moors from North Africa. These invaders were not particularly famous for their good manners, or their respect for local customs and private property. In the thirteenth century the Cathars arrived. These were Christians from the east with unorthodox views, so the Albigensian crusade was launched against them, killing at least a million. The Inquisition finished off the rest. In the seventeenth century the Wars of Religion were replayed, this time with Protestant Huguenots as the enemy and with appalling casualties on both sides.

It's not hard to understand why people built castles and fortresses all over the place. Europe then was pretty much like Afghanistan now. But in the 18th and 19th centuries the ruins left behind by this horror show began to be romanticized. Painters made the old castles look picturesque, poets and writers imagined tales of chivalry and knights in shining armor, although their actual armor was made of iron and was probably more rust colored than shining.

Now the romantic version of history is firmly established, and the region is a picturesque vacation spot for Parisians. Thousands of people come to gaze and photograph and clamber over the crumbling remains of wars that are so far in the past that they have been sanitized by time and ignorance. Indeed, the guide books sometimes fall into the language of Disney and actually talk about "fairy tale castles." I don't know what kind of fairy tales they are thinking about, but the Brothers Grimm come to mind. These ruins are nothing more or less than the relics of two thousand years of barbarism.

Carcassonne is probably the most famous and certainly the most popular of these fairy tale castles. It is basically a nineteenth century restoration in gothic revival style, and it looks magical from a distance. Inside the walls you can see medieval pageants and jousting tournaments, and buy child-sized suits of armor in rust-proof plastic, and outside the walls you can watch a fine *son et lumière* display that is more imaginative than historical.

I suppose that, in the long run, everything that is remembered at all is turned into entertainment and that our present-day "crusader castles" will suffer the same ignominious fate. We can only hope that the tourists who come to see our ruins a thousand years from now will imagine us as knights in shining armor.

Chapter 47

This Year in Odysseum

Fifteen years ago I wrote an essay with the title "The Tram to Odysseum." In it I recounted how my weakness for romantic place names had led me to a strangely disappointing discovery, as so often happens. Just try following the sign that says "Utopia Parkway" on Long Island and see where it gets you. This particular disappointment happened in the French city of Montpellier when I saw a tram gliding by that had on its destination board the irresistible name "Odysseum." I jumped on board at once, without a ticket.

Odysseus was the hero of Homer's *Odyssey*, one of the great travel and adventure stories of all time. Jumping on a French tram without a ticket was exactly the sort of thing that Odysseus would have done. Somehow, in the destination of this tram, the name of Odysseus had been combined with the name of the Greek Paradise – Elysium – to form that infinitely enticing word Odysseum. How could anyone resist?

When my tram reached Odysseum, the end of the line, it was inevitably a let-down. The place was nothing but a gigantic building site, a mega-shopping center in the making. I took the next tram back to town.

Life does go in circles, as you may have noticed. Returning to Montpellier last week we enjoyed a nostalgic visit to a hotel where we had stayed many years ago. It was and is a slightly dilapidated 18th century building that in those days was way out in the country – in fact its name means "House in the Scrubland." What we had failed to realize was that the old hotel had been right on the edge of the new Odysseum, and was now almost engulfed by commercial development. The hotel had kept its old world charm (and, I would swear, the same sandpaper-quality sheets and towels). But beyond the surrounding park shaded by two hundred year old cedars, and only a short walk from the front gates, Odysseum was waiting - a combination of enormous shopping mall, theme park and entertainment center. We had to go and see it, of course.

It was, as expected, one of those huge, hideous commercial centers where the French gift for style and beauty fails so utterly that you feel you are in a different country – not so much landscapes of desire as landscapes of desperation. Everything was there from the Pirates of the Caribbean restaurant experience to McDonalds, Pizza Hut, Subway, hundreds of boutiques selling sneakers and peculiar clothing and a multiplex showing American blockbusters. Teenagers wandered everywhere like lost souls, staring at their phones. In the middle of it all, very mysteriously but perhaps as an homage to Homer, stood a fake Greek temple displaying statues of such ancient Greek heroes as Lenin, Churchill, and Roosevelt.

After a few minutes wandering in this fantasyland we needed some food, and more to the point a drink. Turning a corner beside the Apple store we found ourselves looking at a totally fake-authentic old-fashioned Paris-style *brasserie* with waiters in long white aprons and excellent food. Was it real, or was it a dream? It was hard to tell, although the bill was real enough.

It is difficult to put a label on this kind of experience, but I call it historical vertigo. We left the totally inauthentic and ugly shopping center and walked back to the totally authentic and beautiful eighteenth century hotel, where the receptionist had vanished but the resident dog was pleased to see us. There are times when the eighteenth century seems closer to us than the twenty first. There are times when we would prefer it to be.

Chapter 48

The Senators Speak

A bench in the marketplace is occupied by a regular assembly of not-very-old retired men. They are known as The Senators because all they do is talk, apart from playing the occasional game of *boules* and making frequent trips to the bar which, by a lucky coincidence, is right beside their bench. They passionately discuss the question of early retirement, the strikes and demonstrations in the streets, the deficit, the Middle East, the price of olives and the relative merits of the local wines. At least I think they are talking about these things: they have picturesque local accents that make it difficult to be sure. But nobody else discusses the issues of the day so thoroughly and at such length in any accent. Politicians in Paris or Washington prefer not to discuss them at all.

The Greek *Agora* or marketplace was the cradle of democracy precisely because citizens gathered there to hear and to argue about the things that mattered to them. If the mayor wants to know what is going on in this village he has only to come down to the marketplace and listen to The Senators. That's real democracy, and perhaps democracy only works on the small scale when everyone can join the debate.

Early one morning I arrived at the market and found that the bench of The Senators was empty. Feeling very bold I sat down there for a few minutes, enjoying the sensation of being at the epicenter of village politics, although I could never hope to be elected here. When the Senate is in session the bench is fully occupied from end to end, so I assume that, as in Washington, an incumbent has to fall off before a vacancy occurs.

This is just the kind of modest, down-to-earth senate we need in Washington. A few talkative senior citizens, a rusty bench and some cheap red wine would accomplish everything that the present senate accomplishes, and at infinitely less cost. Their debates might be incomprehensible, confused, irrelevant, and incoherent. But how would we ever tell the difference?

Chapter 49

Counting the Days

Our calendars and appointment books for next year are not yet familiar friends, but they soon will be. I like the spacious feeling that comes from hanging a new calendar. There it is, a whole blank year ahead when anything is possible. There's also the aesthetic aspect. The illustrations on a wall calendar are of primary importance, because we will have to look at them for three hundred and sixty-five days. Last year I had pigs on my office calendar, and very agreeable companions they were. In 2008 it was penguins, and this year it will be cats all the way through to December. It's something to look forward to.

This year we had to make our 2015 wall calendar purchase in France, so we ended up with pictures of food that look very cheerful in the kitchen. The January page shows a delicate plate of savory seafood treats: shrimps with herb seasonings, red caviar with dill and *crème frèche*, fingers of smoked trout, and *Coquilles Saint-Jacques* - a good start to the year.

Along with the calendar I needed a diary (or appointment book, or date book, or personal organizer, or whatever you choose to call these essential memory aids). The French call them "agenda" which sounds rather impressive, as if one actually had an agenda like a corporate governing board or Vladimir Putin. I spent half an hour in the local bookstore last week, making the choice. This little book will be in my hand every day. I want it to look good and feel right, as if I can trust it.

There is a complicated psychological symbolism at work in the design of these agenda books. Size alone is important. Do I really want to admit that my life is so dull that it will fit into one of those tiny pocket-size diaries? Do I feel so busy and important that I need the full 8" x 12" ledger-style diary with a full page for every day? No, that would be embarrassing. For as long as I can remember my annual agenda books have been the same size: eight inches by five. This is the correct size for a reasonable person, suggesting a life that is full enough, but not overloaded with tasks an appointments.

In addition to the crude but simple choice of size there are more subtle decisions to be made: one week on a page, one week across two pages, days arranged vertically or horizontally, and so on. Each choice has consequences. A vertical arrangement of dates, for example, suggests a steady decline, a falling through the day or week, while a horizontal arrangement feels more level and promising. Some diaries have very small spaces for the weekends, suggesting that all the important stuff happens Monday to Friday. But I prefer the weekend days to have exactly the same space as all the rest, or even a little more. It all influences the way we see time: as a kind of *oubliette* into which all things vanish, or as a reassuring progression of one thing after another with no end in sight.

Last, but by no means least, is the question of how your agenda *looks*. After all it is a part of yourself, your portable memory. Here the French excel in design. Their diaries have *panache*. The one I finally chose (in the correct size, give or take a centimeter or two) has a dark red cover with a delicate gold inlay in what the publishers describe as Renaissance style, lots of useful reference pages, and a red silk ribbon to indicate what week it is when I forget. It sounds expensive but it wasn't. There's no battery to run out, no tricky software to learn, and no added gimmicks like a video camera or GPS system. It's just an empty date book that will soon be full, and it will see me through the next twelve months very nicely.

Chapter 50

Winter Winds

D espite the tantalizing promise of global warming we still have to suffer through winter every year. But there is something quite scary about a long spell of cold weather. It's a harsh reminder that we are living on a slightly warm ball of rock in the middle of an infinite space where the temperature is around minus two hundred and fifty degrees centigrade, just a few clicks of the thermostat above absolute zero.

The south of France escapes the worst of the freeze, but everything is relative. Temperatures can sank below zero centigrade at night and hover just above all day. The winter winds blow fiercely, the Tramontane from the northwest and the Mistral from the north, and their poetic names were no consolation.

The first time we spent a winter in France the chill took me back to my childhood in England, in the days when only the rich had central heating. We had a small coal fire in the living room, a stove in the kitchen, and not much heat anywhere else. The fire threw a cone of warmth out into the room, and everybody tried to crowd into it, especially the cat. Being smaller and more agile, the cat usually ended up in the warmest spot, and I was right behind him. We got so close to the flames, the cat and I, that sometimes we were slightly singed. But the moment we stepped away from the fireplace the air was chill, and the door into the hallway was like an airlock leading into Antarctica. The phone was kept in the hallway to discourage long conversations. We moved hastily from slightly warm to freezing cold areas and back again, closing each door firmly behind us to hold what heat there was. Having a bath in winter was torture. Hot water bottles in the bed were a necessity.

Winter in France reminded me strongly of this experience. The house was unevenly heated by small electric radiators that each produced about as much heat as a toaster. But we were well provided with woolen sweaters, socks, and hats. And just before the worst of the cold weather closed in Pascal, our universal handyman, came and installed an impressive device called reversible air conditioning. This system is very popular in Europe. It literally blows hot or cold according to the weather and it apparently works in winter by using a heat pump to convert cold air outside into warm air inside. It seems to me to violate the Second Law of Thermodynamics (you can't transfer heat from a cooler place to a hotter place), not to mention the first law of common sense. But the heater worked beautifully, so I suppose my physics teacher was right to give me a failing grade all those years ago.

With this mysterious machine humming away in a corner the house stayed deliciously warm. But it does raise a moral question that could only be answered by combining the wisdom of a meteorologist, an ethicist, and a physicist. By wringing the last traces of heat out of the already frigid air so that we can be comfortable indoors, are we not making things worse for everybody else?

Chapter 51

Café Society

One of the many myths about the south of France is that the weather is warm and sunny all year round. It isn't. We are just a few miles from the Mediterranean coast and, as I write this, I'm looking out the window at a steady, heavy fall of snow that has been going on for hours. This kind of weather always surprises the locals, who like to believe in their own myth of a sub-tropical paradise. They are completely unprepared for cold weather, although it happens every year. Domestic heating is pathetically inadequate (I have learned to type while wearing gloves), and snow clearance is non-existent. The village snow removal team consists of a man with a bucket of salt that he spreads by hand, and another man on a quad bike with a small shovel. Everyone else is indoors, wearing several layers of clothing, watching the lights flicker on and off. The hardware store in town long ago sold out of kerosene heaters, candles and batteries, as it does every January.

If you want to get warm the best thing is to go to a café. Where there's food and drink you can guarantee that there will be people and heat. France still has a café society in the old-fashioned sense. In most cafés you can choose to drink alcohol or not, and many also have simple meals. They are fairly utilitarian places. Tables tend to be very close together, so there's always the possibility of romance with the woman or man at your elbow. In the small towns and villages, cafes are *the* social centers for adults. The society you find there depends on which establishment you choose. One may be frequented by farmers, one by artists, one by foreign residents, and so on.

These local establishments offer a distant glimpse of what European café society was like in the last century. Cafés were like clubs, where people would gather to talk, read, argue, and play chess. Most elegant were the Viennese cafés, where the glitterati of art, literature and music would go to be seen and to hear all the latest gossip. The famous cafes of Paris, like *Le Café de Flore* and *Les Deux Magots* hosted high-culture celebrities like Hemingway, Sartre, and Picasso. Even London had its pale reflection of café society: part of my youth was misspent in the Partisan Café in Soho, where you could meet political radicals, intellectuals and hippies from all over the world.

Even today, in the French provinces, cafés are places to read, meet, and talk, though not necessarily for intellectuals who are all huddled together in Paris. There are no fantastically-named coffees at fantastic prices, no barristas, and no wi-fi. American coffee bars are different. They tend to be quiet, with customers gazing at their laptops or the tiny screens of their cell phones. If you want to look at the Internet in France you go to a cyber-café, an entirely different type of establishment full of male teenagers wearing hooded anoraks and streaming ultra-violent American television series. They don't understand English, but they don't have to.

The café/bar business has been hit by the smoking ban. But smokers and café owners are nothing if not resourceful. In winter many establishments still have tables set up on the sidewalk under an awning, and each chair is provided with a large, heavy blanket. Even when it's freezing you can find the smokers sitting out there, wrapped up in blankets like Tibetan monks, puffing away on their Gauloises and complaining about the delayed arrival of global warming.

Luckily I'm a non-smoker. I can just plunge into the café, savor the smells and the noise of conversation, and the delicious sensation of being, for the moment, warm.

Chapter 52

The Taste of a French Christmas

The last time we spent Christmas in a French village it was a strange experience. We were accustomed to the American Holiday timetable, which begins with the first gift catalogs in August, and winds up to a pitch of commercial hysteria through September, October and November, before exploding into complete madness in December.

By contrast, nothing seemed to be happening in the village. By December 20 the town hall had been hung with a few colored lights, but that was about it. No house decorations, no special window displays, no Christmas carols being played over loudspeakers. In this, as in other things, the villagers seemed disinclined to go over the top.

This relaxed attitude was something of a relief, but it did make us rather nervous. It was like driving straight at a brick wall in a car with no brakes. After all, The Holidays *were* coming. They could not be stopped. Yet here were these French people, on December 20, strolling around, chatting and casually shopping for bread and onions, as if they didn't have a care in the world.

My theory is that this annoying *insouciance* was caused by the French Revolution. In 1792 the revolutionaries, hoping to erase memories of the old regime, introduced an entirely new calendar, with new names for the months and new festivals. Christmas was *not* included, and Christmas shopping was therefore eliminated. I don't think the French have ever forgotten what a glorious relief this was. Ever since Christmas was restored to their calendar by Napoleon in 1806, they have been rather half-hearted about it.

Years later we spent Christmas in a different French village, and I didn't see much improvement. On December twenty-second, when we arrived, there were a few colored lights strung along the main street, and television was packed with Christmas specials, but the actual population seemed to be ignoring the whole thing. So I determined to discover what was (or was not) going on, gathered a bunch of local newspapers, and headed for the shops, where Christmas is supposed to happen.

It eventually became clear that I had missed the obvious. Christmas in a French village or country town is not about gifts or decorations, or even about religion: it is about *food*. For thousands of years the Winter Solstice celebration has been built around feasting and sociability, a collective effort to push back the darkness and the cold.

The markets and shops were loaded with food in a way that reminded me of the opening chapter of Dickens's *A Christmas Carol*, where he lovingly describes the cornucopia of food on display in Victorian London on Christmas Eve. Here were mountains of live oysters, a favorite Christmas dish, along with hams and *patés*, *foie gras*, *pintades*, mushrooms, cheeses, snails, olives, and of course tens of thousands of bottles of local wine. The village butcher's shop was a vegetarian's chamber of horrors, with just about every part of every edible bird and animal on display, and some creatures we couldn't identify at all but didn't like to ask.

The local newspapers reported Christmas celebrations in three categories: parties for children, featuring Father Christmas, and food, community events with music and food, and parties for senior citizens with nothing but food. Most villages also have special Christmas markets in December, and there's no need to describe what they sell.

We had barely recovered from this gastronomic marathon when it was time to celebrate the New Year, which in secular France is a much more significant festival than Christmas. I bet you can't guess what they did to celebrate the New Year.

Chapter 53

So What's Special About France?

France is the only large country in the world that has more visitors a year than its total population. Italy or Sweden or Germany or Poland don't have the same cachet, perhaps because so many Americans came from those countries. But the French, with a few exceptions, have stayed at home, which makes them more mysterious. They think France is the best place to be, and so do many foreigners. Apart from the tourists, generations of intellectuals, artists and writers like F. Scott Fitzgerald, Henry Miller, Samuel Becket have headed to France in pursuit of some Holy Grail of culture.

What do the rest of us hope to find in France? It is a visually beautiful country of course, but no more so than many others. The language is impossible, the culture tends to exclude outsiders, and the political scene is confusing and annoying. Yet in some ways, it is a model of what a modern country can be. The French have somehow managed to embrace both socialism and capitalism. They are good at capitalism, but long ago decided that some things are too important to be trusted to for-profit corporations. Breakfast cereal or TV reality shows can safely be left to the business sector, because they don't touch the fundamental quality of life. But the things that matter are basic housing, health care, public transport, and education, which should be available to everyone and should never, ever be left to the mercy of private interests. This shifts the balance of society in a dramatic way. Work and money are less important, and family, leisure, and culture are more important. The government is responsible for so much that it can be blamed for almost everything, which pleases everyone.

It is an inescapable cliché to say that France is a mixture of old and new. It is a nation of ancient villages, agricultural landscapes, and traditional habits. At the same time it has a dynamic modern economy, the third largest in Europe and sixth in the world. It is a manufacturer of world class cars and aircraft, and Paris fashions set the standard for all the rest. It is the world's leading producer of nuclear power and has Europe's largest space program. A French company, Sodexho, is one of the largest food service providers in America, and feeds the American army abroad. Accor runs almost four thousand international hotels, and Hachette is the third largest book publisher in the world. All this is quite impressive in a small country, especially when you remember that the French have a thirty-five hour week and six weeks paid holiday. But still their GDP per hour worked is higher than in America, and GDP per worker is about the same.

In France you find a super high tech and a traditional world side by side. The dynamic modern economy and strong social safety net allow people to be more relaxed and adventurous in their lives. They spend much more time with their families than Americans do, and they routinely choose more leisure time over more disposable income. It's not paradise, but no place with human beings is. Even paradise itself stopped being paradise when a couple of people arrived.

Another French advantage is the relatively low profile of religion. France has been a formally secular society since 1905, when the separation of church and state was established. So religion is largely irrelevant and politics is very ideological in a secular way. There are big arguments over basic issues. Debate tends to be very intense and very anarchic. As General de Gaulle once asked: "How can anyone govern a country that has two hundred and forty-six kinds of cheese?"

I have often thought that the French really enjoyed their revolution, chaotic and anarchic though it was. They have never quite got over it. You can tell by the way they drive and park that the spirit of anarchy is not dead. Evading government regulations is practically a patriotic duty. And there's a fierce patriotism that appears on occasions like Bastille Day that makes a foreigner feel just a bit out of place.

French journalists and intellectuals obsess over the problem of foreign influence, and the question of national identity. French culture is not a rigid, old-fashioned or isolated. It is changing fast. The popular culture is obsessed with American themes. Even the distinguished newspaper *Le Monde* crams its pages with reviews of American novels, movies and art. This worries those who would like to see France as a nation unique in the world, and who fear that its identity is being lost.

In my opinion, they have plenty of identity, almost too much. Nobody can be French like the French, or remind you so often that you are *not* French, which they see as a misfortune rather than a fault. Even in the face of American TV series, McDonalds, and the invasion of foreigners like us who buy houses here, French culture is in no danger from us.

What is special about France for me is that being here gives the pleasant illusion of living in the past and the present at the same time. I can lie in bed listening to the bells from the clock tower, aware of the almost medieval darkness and silence of the night, and thinking about tomorrow's market or the walk we may take, or a place we have visited. At the same time I know that if anything goes wrong I could be whisked away by a state of the art car into a state of the art hospital. This feeling of living two lives at once suggests that we are somehow cheating time itself – and what could be more satisfying than that? For me, as for many others, France offers a parallel and richer life that I can't quite fully possess, but can inhabit like a rented house in a beautiful landscape. I must have dimly realized this from the moment of my first encounter with cassoulet and leek and potato soup on a wet night in Reims in 1957. Everyone is entitled to their own particular version of nostalgia, and that's mine. All I ask from France is to be surprised and delighted, and France delivers every time.

About The Author

David Bouchier began rambling around France on his motor cycle in the nineteen sixties, and is still rambling. He worked as a journalist and bookseller in London, and as a tour guide in Greece and Turkey. Later he received a PhD from the London School of Economics, and spent two decades teaching sociology at universities in Britain.

Marriage to an American citizen, plus an ardent desire to escape the British climate, brought David to the United States as a visiting professor at the State University of New York before changing tracks to become a freelance writer and broadcaster.

His humor column "Out of Order" appeared in the regional Sunday edition of *The New York Times* for ten years, and he has contributed fiction and non-fiction to many literary and political magazines. On radio he has established a distinctively ironic voice with his weekly essays on National Public Radio stations in New York and Connecticut, and was also the popular host of a program of classical music and commentary on the same stations.

David lives alternately in Stony Brook, Long Island, and in a village near Uzès in France, with his wife Diane, a retired professor and artist, and various visiting cats.

Made in the USA
Lexington, KY
22 December 2015